HERESY HUNTERS

Character Assassination in the Church

JAMES R. SPENCER

Huntington House Publishers

Huntington House Publishers
P.O. Box 53788
Lafayette, Louisiana 70505

Library of Congress Card Catalog Number 93-77321
ISBN 1-56384-042-1

ALSO BY JAMES R. SPENCER

Beyond Mormonism: An Elder's Story
Have You Witnessed to a Mormon Lately?
Hard Case Witnessing: Winning "Impossibles" for Christ
The Mormon Dilemma (video, co-authored with
Ed Decker)

To contact James R. Spencer or to receive the newsletter "Through the Maze," write:

James R. Spencer
"Through the Maze"
P. O. Box 8656
Boise, ID 83707

To my loving wife, Margaretta, who encourages me to keep preaching and who is a source of wisdom, insight, and counsel.

I offer heartfelt thanks to the following friends: Alex Ohlsen, Tim Moen, Dan Ferguson, and Lenny Meyer, four pastors who helped me think through the spiritual implications of this project and who forced me to clarify my thinking; Tim Dart for his important manuscript work, especially in the earlier chapters; Rusty Downey for responding to a desperate call for computer keyboard help; and Richard Phelps for supplying me with documents without which this project could not have been completed. I am also indebted to the *Tulsa Christian Times* for inspiration for the opening paragraphs of chapter 2, and to Wells Bradly who provided me with court transcripts.

This book would be incomplete without valuable input from Glenn Miles, who helped me understand the philosophical perspective of the heresy hunters. Dick Landis saved me from the sin of excess in chapter 6. Alan and Harriet Henderson provided important encouragement, as did the loyal supporters of "Through the Maze."

Erin Hansen, my daughter, not only spent numerous hours at the computer, but she also provided invaluable insight and suggestions. She, along with my wife, really made this a team project.

Finally, my wife, Margaretta, released me to be a part-time husband/father/grandfather during the final weeks of this effort. She also rescued me from the temptation to end the book without calling heresy hunters to repentance.

Heresy hunters, beware! The mask is off in this critical evaluation of the character assassins within and without the Church. James Spencer, who comes from an analytical journalist background, shines the light of truth on self-appointed judges who "sow discord among brethren." Innumerable evils have torn the Body of Christ and all in the name of "doctrinal purity." But the immediate question that calls for an answer is WHOSE DOCTRINE? As I have said so often, one theologian's heresy is another theologian's orthodoxy. The heretic hunters' favorite Scripture is: "Earnestly contend for the faith which was once delivered unto the saints" (Jude 3).

So what is "the faith"? The answer is simple; read it in the Apostle's Creed or any number of other confessions such as the Heidelberg Confession: Jesus Christ, born of a virgin, crucified, risen again, ascended to heaven, by whose blood our sins are forgiven, who will return in power and glory to judge the living and the dead. Beyond these absolute essentials of "FAITH," there is infinite room for honest men and women to disagree and debate the limitless issues of "doctrinal purity." Indeed, Paul Billheimer, our beloved Wesleyan Methodist writer, put forward a most interesting thesis in his classic book, *Love Covers*. He reasoned as follows:

> In the area of doctrine essential to our eternal salvation, scripture is so clear that we have no significant disagreement within the Body of Christ in this area.

"That if thou shall confess with thy mouth the Lord Jesus, and believe in thine heart that God hath raised him from the dead, thou shalt be saved. For with the heart man believeth unto righteousness; and with the mouth confession is made unto salvation" (Rom. 10:9-10).

However, in other areas of doctrine, Scripture is not as clear. "Why?" asks Paul Billheimer. His answer is certainly worthy of serious and honest consideration. The reason: God deliberately left some things for us, the Body of Christ, to work out between ourselves in agape love. This would, in effect, force the true Body of Christ to come together as one in "the faith." Some of this controversy has, in fact, ended to a great degree. The disagreements over "eternal security" and "tongues," for example, have faded into blessed obscurity. But—enter the spoilers who James Spencer aptly identifies as the "heresy hunters." Their witch-hunts and character assassinations never end. And it is right there that we should identify the difference between a true "apologist," who is an honest seeker of truth, from the "heretic hunters." The true apologist raises questions and issues of doctrine, even calling certain doctrine into question as heretical, but NEVER judging a brother or sister by name with whom he may disagree. If a true apologist has a controversy with a fellow believer, he goes to that one privately and attempts to work it out in Christian love. Many times the issue is settled, and both may learn and receive new light on the issue. If not, fellow believers should simply agree to disagree as long as the issue or doctrine is nonessential to one's eternal salvation. I once asked a great saint of God, Edgar Bethany, this question: Why do honest and sincere men of faith often disagree on matters of nonessential doctrine? His answer has helped me to better understand this perplexing question. He said,

> Son, if you could observe and talk to three individuals traveling on foot to a yonder city, one, ten miles distance, the next, five miles distant, and the next, only one mile distant, and you asked them to report

what they saw, you would get three very different answers. The one ten miles distant would say, "I see only light on the horizon." The second may say, "I see very bright light and the outline of landmarks and buildings." The one only one mile distant might say, "I see tall buildings, street lights, automobiles, and people moving about." Each traveler is reporting honestly what he is observing, but because of the differing proximity to the city, the descriptions would vary considerably. So it is with our Christian faith. We are all pilgrims journeying to a distant city, but we are all at different points of proximity along the way, so we may not always agree on the description of that city.

As stated earlier, men and women of goodwill can agree to disagree on nonessential doctrines on the way to the "city." When we get there the true believers should have worked it out in agape love and, if not, the Lord Himself will reveal to all who was right or wrong. But not so with the heresy hunters. They continue to slash and burn, question motives, call individual character into question, and sit as judge and jury on their fellow believers. They continue to "burn at the stake" all with whom they disagree on their TV and radio programs and in their books and newsletters.

Let us, the Body of Christ, cry out to the heretic hunters:

> Dear brothers, YOU ARE ATTACKING THE WRONG ENEMY! The enemy is the Devil and his gang of apostates. If you have to attack something, there are plenty of false cults, false religions, New Age, secular humanism, and damnable heresies of all kinds. Let us cry out to the heretic hunters to join us in the "good fight of faith" against the REAL enemy instead of dissipating all their energy wrangling over whether we are "little gods" or not.

Let us pray that James Spencer's book will be the wake up call to all the Body of Christ that we can be one and

will someday be ONE as Jesus prayed in John 17. To that
end I commend this book to the precious Body of Christ
with the prayer that that day will be soon

Paul F. Crouch, President
Trinity Broadcasting Network

Give a warm welcome to any brother who wants to
join you, even though his faith is weak. Don't criticize
him for having different ideas from yours about what
is right and wrong. They are God's servants, not yours.
They are responsible to Him, not you. Let Him tell
them whether they are right or wrong. And God is
able to make them do as they should." (Rom. 14:1, 4
Living Bible)

A heresy hunter, by the definition I use in this book, does not really hunt heresy; he hunts people. I am not "after" anybody in this book. I have, of necessity, used real examples in this book. Such a book as this could not be written theoretically. In using real examples to illustrate my actual target—the error of heresy hunting—I could not avoid "naming names." As I say within the pages of this book, I do not think naming names is the issue. Rather, it is *how* and *why* we name names.

I want heresy hunters to stop their ungodly activity. However, in an attempt to get them to do that, I am not trying to discredit any one of them or to make an example of them. I simply tell the story of those who have been hunted, and in so doing, I could not avoid naming the hunters. To do so would have created a painful, fractured book that, in the end, would not have protected the identities of the heresy hunters anyway.

I would never have written such a book were it not necessary to defend Christian ministers. I am aware that such a disclaimer will not prevent me from being charged with doing the same thing I am accusing the heresy hunters of doing. But the fact that I find myself involved in a controversy does not mean I started the controversy; if a man commits a crime, you can't accuse the defense attorney of starting a fight.

Some things cannot be avoided. For too long I have watched silently as the strategy and tactics of modern heresy hunters became so outlandish that I felt I had to respond or be a coward. I hope this book will serve to reduce the debilitating blood-letting so that we can get on with the job of winning God's beloved lost ones to Christ.

The modern heresy hunters I challenge in this book are attempting to hang the label "heretic" on individuals who, in my opinion, are not heretics. If I'm wrong, then those I am calling heresy hunters really have done us a service. God will eventually sort everything out. In the meantime, all I can do is say what I believe. I only want my brothers who have been maligned to be allowed to continue their ministries without the interference of misguided critics.

CHAPTER 1

Friendly Fire

To the non-believers, the scene was pandemonium and hysteria: people were sprawled across pews; others stood riveted in place while their bodies shook uncontrollably (they were said to have "the jerks"); others repeatedly jumped up and down in place. One woman lay on her back and rolled from side to side, her arms stretched up to heaven and her eyes fixed on the ceiling of the church. Listening closely, you could hear her softly moan, "Jesus, Jesus, Jesus." Others fainted, and still others danced and leaped in what they described as "ecstasy."

The next day a group of pastors hotly debated the meeting. Some thought it was a genuine outpouring of God. Others were disgusted, saying the meeting was nothing more than an emotional exhibition, a blight on the Church. Suddenly the group was interrupted by a slender, middle-aged man with wavy hair that hung to his shoulders. As he walked quietly into the room, all eyes were on him, some pleading for an explanation, others glaring with disgust. A few men simply turned their eyes down to the open Bibles on their laps and waited for the minister to speak.

The controversial church meeting did not take place in Tulsa or the Ozarks. It was not a Pentecostal tent meeting, nor was it orchestrated by a flashy televangelist. On the contrary, the extraordinary meeting took place within a stately, stained-glass-windowed church in New England. It was one of numerous other meetings exactly

13

like it which occurred throughout New England between the 1730s and 1740—the period historians call the Great Awakening.

The architect of the Great Awakening—and the minister who would attempt to explain its unusual manifestation to his skeptical colleagues—was a highly respected Congregational pastor named Jonathan Edwards. The Great Awakening is heralded as one of the most important outpourings of God ever to shake America. Its implications still affect American society. It supplied the American colonists with the courage to wage the Revolutionary War. It wove a moral fabric into the Constitution. It laid a godly foundation for our national spirit. Nevertheless, the Great Awakening had its critics. Some of its supernatural elements were simply too much for Christians who had been converted to Christ under other, less dramatic circumstances. The New England populace was not used to such emotional displays.

The controversy over the Great Awakening was to be expected. Historically, revival has been—for lack of a better word—messy. When God supernaturally invades human society, two things occur: first, sleepy Christians are frightened by the genuine enthusiasm of fresh heavenly fire; and second, counterfeit spiritual manifestations haunt the genuine outpouring.

The first reaction by carnal Christians to the vibrancy of genuine spirituality has always been skepticism. And skepticism has led to splits, factions, and denominationalism. Historically, the Church has had a tendency to lose its first love and become cold. New, vibrant Christians strain against the old guard until a new group or denomination is formed.

The second reaction to revival is that other (unconverted) people begin to mimic the genuine manifestations. Sometimes people are attracted to the spiritual power which accompanies revivals; sometimes demonized people show up. Satan hopes to dampen the revival and to introduce error. Wherever God is moving, you may be sure the devil is active. As one evangelist has said, "Where there is light, there will be bugs!"

The Great Awakening was not perfectly pure; some of the manifestations were less than truly spiritual. Some contained genuine error. Sorting the genuine from the counterfeit was difficult.

In addition to honest theological critics—men motivated by the highest principles who moved with care and godliness, a hoard of ungodly critics indiscriminately attacked—not only the revival, but the men and women whom God raised up for His work. Self-appointed guardians of the faith—themselves unspiritual—savaged anointed ministries, and jealous faultfinders invented evil reports—all in the name of God.

The revival slowed and eventually ended under a barrage of criticism from hair-splitting, theological nit-pickers. The Great Awakening, like all revivals, eventually died. Tragically, the revival was, at least in part, destroyed from within.

The Rise of the Modern Heresy Hunter

Our century has produced two periods of revival, both of which were as historically significant as the Great Awakening. The first was the Pentecostal Revival that began with the turn of this century. The second was the Charismatic Renewal that began in the 1950s and lasted until the early 1980s.

The Charismatic Renewal occurred, however, in an age far different from the other American revivals. Ours is a thoroughly secularized society; it has been described as "post-Christian." Actually, a more accurate term would be "post-theistic." Modern society is quick to condemn anything that is overtly Christian, that is "fundamentalist" Christian or "evangelical" Christian.

A second difference between the Great Awakening and the modern revivals is the modern communication revolution. Not only are radio and television radical new communication forms, but they also dictate how we communicate. We have been reduced to communicating thoughts in the form of headlines, pictures, and sound-bites. I will discuss the communications revolution in greater detail in the next chapter.

Modern heresy hunters exhibit many of the same characteristics similar to those of earlier ages; they stalk the modern revival the way their forefathers did the Great Awakening. Today, however, the self-appointed guardians of the Church are armed with cameras and desktop publishing equipment. Today everything happens at light-speed. Well-meaning but unwise Christians quickly upload damning information to huge numbers of people. Christian doctrine used to be mulled over in pastors' studies and seminaries and passed on to the Church over a period of years through pulpits; today, doctrinal ideas are traded like baseball cards, theological ideas are sold like laundry soap, and preachers are promoted like political candidates.

In such an age well-intentioned Christian critics, writers, and radio and television talk-show hosts are often tempted to make negative claims about ministries, claims that turn out to be erroneous. Unwise but articulate "experts" can readily get the ear of thousands of Christians and spread half-baked ideas about the theological positions of fellow ministers. Sometimes their research is shoddy and their tactics questionable.

All this has introduced modern hazards to preaching the gospel. Modern evangelists are falling under a barrage of what we call "friendly fire." We saw an example of friendly fire during the Gulf War when American forces inadvertently destroyed an armored personnel carrier full of British soldiers. Today such casualties within the Christian community are at an all time high. If unchecked, I believe this trend will escalate to produce one of the most violent divisions in the Church's history.

I call these new, self-appointed watchdogs "heresy hunters." The current environment allows nit-pickers and bean-counters to masquerade as scholars. It allows men and women of partial vision to move into arenas beyond their wisdom. A world in which exposé is commonplace has produced a climate in which a book can undo a minister overnight. The very way in which the charges are brought against him is sometimes enough to cause people to jump to the ill-founded conclusions of the heresy hunter.

Of course, the Church still needs genuine, godly critics. However, genuine apologists not only defend the faith but they also defend the brethren—even those who may need correction. The heresy hunters possess a vision so narrowed to their own brand of Christian experience that they cannot recognize the difference between heretics and fellow ministers. While both apologists and heresy hunters may be motivated by a sincere desire to protect the Church from error, heresy hunters divide the Church by defaming legitimate brothers and sisters in Christ.

In my opinion, an alarming error is sweeping the Church. Heresy hunters first identify those they believe are not worthy to minister and then mount public relations campaigns to remove the unworthy ministers. I believe this is both unbiblical and ungodly.

Spiritual Discernment

The nature of Christianity certainly requires us to be careful. No one argues with that. A certain amount of healthy skepticism is essential. Scripture warns us repeatedly about false prophets who will arise among us and introduce false doctrines and practices. Time and time again, Jesus Himself—as well as the Apostles Peter, John, and Paul—commanded us to watch out for false brethren and challenge the demonic doctrines they bring.

We cannot be too vigilant in our task. Heresy isn't just wrong; it is soul-destroying. Spiritual error produces mutated fruit. Jim Jones and David Koresh led hundreds of people to their suicidal deaths; Joseph Smith and Brigham Young led thousands into the horrors of polygamy and blood atonement; Mary Baker Eddy led other thousands to a perverted, New Age Jesus.

Since Christianity is the answer for man's fallen soul, the enemy of our soul—Satan—has set himself up to destroy the Gospel. One of his most effective methods is to pervert the Gospel, to change it in its essential parts while leaving the structure intact. Therefore, error which rises from within the Church is much more difficult to spot than, say, error from the Eastern religions. The devil knows it is sometimes easier to pervert true Christianity than to import a wholly new religious experience.

The division between genuine spiritual experience and the counterfeit is often hairline thin. Who is qualified to judge in these matters? What criteria must be used? How do we uproot evil without throwing out the baby with the bath water? Who dares to speak for God? Who will say this minister is qualified to preach and that one is not?

These are tough questions; the answers are not simple. If we do not answer them correctly, we may make the mistake of overlooking destructive errors that will poison and destroy the people of God. On the other hand, if we are too quick to attack what looks like heresy, but which is not, we can suddenly find ourselves in opposition to God, working to destroy men and women He has appointed to be instruments of ministry in His hands.

In addition, if we mistakenly condemn ministers God has not condemned, we risk destroying not only them but their effective ministry as well. This means that we have to stand for both love as well as truth. This balance between truth and love is delicate. It is important to me, personally. For nearly twenty years I have fought against heresy. I was saved out of a cult (Mormonism). After ten years in pastoral ministry, I moved into full-time ministry to the people caught in the cults, the occult, and secularism.

One of the things I have learned is that "cult-busters," like myself, can sometimes be too harsh. Therefore, I have adopted as the watchword of my ministry this saying: "Truth without love is too hard; love without truth is too soft." Or, as a pastor friend recently paraphrased, "Love without truth is just mush; truth without love is brutal."

My concern is that many would-be apologists seem to be unable to understand the foundational charge Christ gave Christians to be forgiving and charitable as well as right. Heresy hunters are firing indiscriminately at "friendly" troops.

Heresy Hunting Today

Four men who have been victims of heresy hunters come quickly to my mind. I will deal with each of them in greater detail in subsequent chapters. They are Benny Hinn, Kenneth Copeland, Bob Larson, and Mike Warnke.

These men are controversial. They are flamboyant, vocal, and "in the face" of the world. These men typify what the world has always scorned in popular ministers. Because of their finger-in-your-face style, they are easy to stereotype. The secular press has spared little effort to characterize them as fringe-area Christian ministers at best and money-grubbing charlatans at worst. These outspoken ministers are nose to nose with the world. In that respect they stand in the shadow of past controversial evangelists like Billy Sunday, Aimee Semple McPherson, and more recently, Oral Roberts.

It is not unusual for Bible-thumpers to be at odds with the world. That is to be expected. What is unusual about these men is that they have been severely attacked by fellow evangelicals.

• Benny Hinn, who pastors the seven thousand-member Orlando Christian Center, is an example of someone who has, in my opinion, been unfairly attacked. He has, for example, been repeatedly called a heretic by a well-known Christian apologetic ministry. I've been shocked by the tone of the attack. I believe the assault on Benny Hinn has far exceeded the bounds of godly criticism and doctrinal disagreement. He has been publicly characterized as outside the Body of Christ and dangerous to the cause of Christ. All these charges are based on a handful of statements made in his books and television sermons that his critics have taken out of context.

• Kenneth Copeland is one of the so-called Word/Faith Teachers. One heresy hunter called him "the worst of all heretics." He supposedly teaches that Christians all should expect to have "unlimited health and unlimited

wealth." But has he been fairly accused? I don't think so.
I believe his remarks have been taken out of context and
he has been made to appear to believe things he doesn't
really believe.

• Bob Larson, who hosts the nationally syndicated radio
talk show, "Talk Back," has always been a subject of controversy. However, a series of articles about him in Christian magazines far exceeded good taste. Some of the attack on Larson resulted from the publication of his novel,
Dead Air, which he wrote to expose what he believes is
widespread Satanism in America. *Cornerstone*, a Christian
magazine, did a series of articles that characterized Larson
as a crackpot and his work as "Christian pornography."
One article was particularly cruel, sophomoric, and em-
barrassing. The author was not so much concerned with
correcting Larson's facts or theology as in humiliating
him and portraying his ministry as simply laughable.

• Probably the saddest example of heresy hunting was
the 1991 smear of the life and ministry of Mike Warnke.
It's true that Warnke was a minister in trouble when his
life was turned upside down by a 30,000-word exposé in
the above-mentioned magazine, *Cornerstone*. It's also true
that Warnke was in trouble of his own making. He was
unquestionably guilty of much of what his accusers claimed.
Nevertheless, the way in which he was prosecuted, convicted, and sentenced was shameful.

What Makes Heresy Hunters Tick?

I have spent untold hours thinking and praying about
the heresy hunter phenomenon. As I have watched ministers brutalized and their work dismantled by well-
intentioned zealots who moved without biblical wisdom,
I have asked, "Why?" Ministers, of course, expect to be
misunderstood and attacked by the world, but they never
understand ruthless attacks from those who are fellow
ministers. I have continued to marvel, "How easily they
lay hands on their brothers!"

I do not know all of the motives of the heresy hunters. I can't see into their hearts. Part of me clings to the hope that they are simply unwise and misguided. However, my investigation causes me to believe that their problems are deeper than that.

In attempting to understand heresy hunters, it may be helpful to take into consideration that Hinn, Copeland, Larson, and Warnke share some common characteristics. For one thing, they are all flamboyant; they have a sense of the dramatic. Larson and Warnke are admitted showmen; they operate in the entertainment industry. Larson hosts a daily national radio talk show, and Warnke bills himself as a Christian comedian. Hinn, meanwhile, traces his ministry roots to Kathryn Kuhlman. He was saved in one of her crusades, and his ministry is reminiscent of her dramatic style.

These men are also connected by Pentecostal or Charismatic doctrinal positions; all believe that God still grants Christians the New Testament "gifts of the Spirit" in order to facilitate ministry.

A third connection is their mutual belief that demons commonly afflict human beings. All of them regularly rebuke the devil as though Satan is a real and present threat. They see a rising tide of Satanism sweeping the nation. They believe the devil, demons, and the realm of the occult are not primarily theological concepts but the stuff of everyday life. Satan is not only alive and well on planet Earth; he is in ever increasing control of much of the everyday activity of human beings.

The flamboyance of these men, their Pentecostal persuasion, and their tumultuous, undignified wrestling with the powers of darkness may be part of the explanation for the attacks on them. In fact, such views may account for the lion's share of all recent heresy hunting. However, I hasten to add that heresy hunters attack non-Pentecostals too. One thing is certain: those under attack are considered by their attackers to be unworthy to minister. Further, the heresy hunters are determined to take the "heretical" brethren out of ministry for good.

Back to the Future

The Great Awakening of Jonathan Edward's day, like every other mighty move of God throughout the history of the Christian Church, was characterized by two phenomena: first, the outpouring was accompanied by spiritual fireworks; and secondly, it was zealously attacked by well-meaning brethren. In fact, the rising tide of opposition to the Great Awakening may well have caused its end.

Modern heresy hunters scrutinize the flamboyant, messy, emotional, hyper-spiritual atmosphere which has characterized not only the recent Charismatic Renewal but also much of the ministry of Christian television. They do so with apparent revulsion. It may be true that some of what they see is carnal. It would be surprising if that were not the case; after all, spiritual treasures are contained in earthen vessels. However, the real question is simply this: has God commissioned the heresy hunters to attack these ministries?

Remember, I am not questioning whether or not the heresy hunters can disagree with these men. Of course they can. I am not questioning whether or not the heresy hunters can write and speak in opposition to the doctrines of these men. Of course they can. I'm questioning only whether the heresy hunters have the right to discipline these men through public censure. Do they have the right to malign them, to publicly declare them to be outside the church? I do not think they do. When they do so, I think they are in grave error.

Jonathan Edwards had to face these same issues. He recognized that excesses did occur within the revival of the Great Awakening. Much of the emotional hype was nothing more than that. People, caught up in the fervor of the moment, often mimicked others. Charlatans hung around the meetings for their own selfish purposes.

On the other hand, Edwards also knew that many of the experiences were genuine—strange, but genuine. God, he concluded, did things in His own way and did not seem to be troubled when He was frequently misunderstood. Edwards also knew that wherever God was moving, Satan would be attempting to promote confusion.

Jonathan Edwards was as interested as anyone else in purity of doctrine. He was a first class scholar whose work still stands as a testimony to his soundness. But even more than he wanted technical purity, he wanted the wind of the Spirit to continue to blow. He sought wisdom in dealing with the uncontrollable fire which drove the revival. He constantly faced down the critics of the Awakening because he knew a secret of God that the critics did not know: God often uses foolish things to confound the wise and learned (1 Cor. 1:27; Matt. 11:25; Luke 10:21).

At the peak of the controversy, Jonathan Edwards preached the commencement sermon at Yale on the subject, "The Distinguishing Marks of a Work of the Spirit of God." In that address he exhorted his fellow ministers to sort the wheat from the chaff in the revival. He argued that the temporary "enthusiasm," even in its unseemly form, was incidental to the true move of God. Edwards, in that speech, set forth his defense for the Great Awakening in spite of its many detractors. Marks of a true move of God, he said, would include raising the esteem of Jesus in the community, working against the kingdom of Satan, and establishing a greater regard for the Bible. In spite of its flaws, the net effect of the Great Awakening was to establish faith in Christ, hatred for the devil, and respect for the Bible.

Conclusion

In my opinion, the modern rise in heresy hunting constitutes a new Inquisition. Heresy hunters who blindly attack their fellow ministers strike at the central unity of the Body of Christ. In so doing, they may become the real heretics themselves.

God hates attacks on His Church. The Bible condemns backbiting in the most serious terms:

These six things doth the Lord hate: yea, seven are an

abomination unto him: A proud look, a lying tongue,
and hands that shed innocent blood, an heart that
deviseth wicked imaginations, feet that be swift in
running to mischief, a false witness that speaketh lies,
and he that soweth discord among brethren. (Prov.
6:16-19)

CHAPTER 2

Feeding Frenzy

Millions of people watched "Prime Time Live's" scathing exposé of three television evangelists in November of 1991. Those who missed it were treated to a review in July of 1992. So convincing was the report that virtually all viewers, from atheists to born-again Christians, bought it as wholly true. The report focused on Larry Lea, pastor of the Church on the Rock in Dallas; Robert Tilton, pastor of Word of Faith Church in Dallas; and W. V. Grant, whom "Prime Time Live" introduced as "an old-fashioned singing revival preacher." The three televangelists were pictured as cold-hearted, money-grubbing preachers who fleeced tens of thousands of people out of millions of dollars.

The report was so convincing that the attorney general of the state of Texas filed a lawsuit against Tilton to rescind Word of Faith's corporate charter, dissolve its ministry, and take over its assets. I, like countless others, watched the program with sadness. I assumed that the information presented was correct. I resigned myself to the fact that three more preachers had fallen.

The worst charges were against Robert Tilton, whom Diane Sawyer, "Prime Time's" anchorwoman, accused of being a total fraud, of fleecing his audience out of "millions of tax free dollars." They also spent a lot of time trying to demonstrate that Tilton had not fulfilled his promise to "pray over" the prayer requests mailed to him.

Instead, "Prime Time Live" said, Tilton never looked at
his mail, but simply had the money from his faithful
donors deposited in his bank account. In the introduction
Sawyer said:

> You've never met anyone quite like Robert Tilton
> before. He heads today's fastest-growing TV ministry.
> He takes in millions of tax-free dollars. . . You'll see
> how the businessman deposits followers' money di-
> rectly into the bank but has a shocking place for their
> prayers and dreams.[1]

The shocking place for their prayer requests, Sawyer
said, was the dumpster behind the main branch of Tulsa's
Commercial Bank and Trust. "Prime Time's" cameras pictured the bank, its trash dumpster, and the Tilton mail,
which Sawyer said "Prime Time" found in the bank's
trash.

Tilton, of course, denied the claims. He admitted his
mail had gone first to his bank, but, he said, that was only
to prevent him or any of his staff from handling it so they
would be free from charges of financial mismanagement.
He claimed the mail was delivered by the U. S. Postal
Service to his bank, where it was opened under scrupu-
lous supervision, the money removed, and the amount of
the donation recorded on each piece of mail. Then the
mail was forwarded to another accounting firm, Internal
Data Management, where donations were recorded, and
where all requests for books, tapes, and Bibles were filled.
IDM then express-mailed the prayer requests to Word of
Faith. A staff minister at Tilton's headquarters has testi-
fied that he would then take the prayer requests directly
to Tilton's home and put them in his "prayer closet." He
said Tilton prayed over all the mail. Later, the letters were
removed to his garage and eventually discarded.

How, then, can one account for the footage of the
mail allegedly found in the dumpster of Commercial Bank's
downtown office? Is it possible that "Prime Time" man-
aged the news and, in effect, staged the news? In fact, that
is exactly what happened.

It turns out that "Prime Time Live" was led to the Tilton story by a man named Ole Anthony, an outspoken "minister" who has a personal vendetta against televangelists in general and Tilton in particular. Anthony went undercover with "Prime Time" to gain secret camera footage of an interview with IDM. Anthony gathered mountains of information on Tilton, including many pieces of Tilton's direct mail advertising. It is probable that it was this mail that wound up being photographed in the "Prime Time" report.

Getting a video copy of both the November 1991 and July 1992 "Prime Time" shows was not easy. I had obtained a copy of the printed transcripts of the July show from Journal Graphics (a company that sells transcripts of televised programs to the public) but was told I could not get the November edition. They said that ABC would only release the July video, insisting it was "identical" to the November program. Apparently, ABC was reluctant to give people the ability to compare the two shows. I finally obtained the November video through a company called "News Tracks" in Tulsa, Oklahoma.

When you run the videos side by side, you see they are far from identical. Many changes have been made, but the most striking is the section which contains the dumpster shots. These have been changed for a very good reason: the earlier video showed a trash dumpster at a bank where Tilton has not had an account for five years! When the chairman of the board of Commercial Bank presented an affidavit stating Tilton had no accounts at the downtown branch, "Prime Time" produced a revised version of the report. The subsequent "Prime Time" program—the July 1992 version—edited out the downtown dumpster footage and showed instead the dumpster at the bank's Peoria branch where Tilton's account is handled. It also replaced the shot of the front of the downtown bank with a shot of the Peoria branch.

What is obvious is that "Prime Time" did not shoot the mail as it came out of the dumpster at all! It shot a dumpster, then shot pictures of Tilton's mail, and then Diane Sawyer *said* the mail came from the dumpster. However, if she didn't even know which bank Tilton used, it is certain the mail shown in the video did not come from the bank's dumpster.

Staging the News

This is called staging the news. The practice is common among the news networks. Recently, NBC news publicly repented of a similar incident. The network admitted staging the explosion of a GMC pickup truck as it was struck by a Chevy Citation. The report was supposed to document that the pickups were unsafe because of the way the gas tanks were mounted. But NBC admitted to planting model rocket-motors under the bottom of the trucks and detonating them at the moment of impact. They also fitted the fuel tanks with the wrong gas caps—loose-fitting caps that would fly off on impact, allowing the gas to spew out. When the rocket motors were detonated, it produced a violent (and very graphic) fireball. When NBC broadcast the exposé, people started parking their trucks and suing GMC. But later, NBC admitted to staging the scene. The fiasco led to the eventual resignation of the president of NBC's news department.

The "Prime Time" exposé of the televangelists is full of similar manipulative tactics. It was motivated by the network's prejudiced position that Bible-thumping evangelists are fools, liars, and money-grubbers. The piece was not simply an indictment of Lea, Grant, and Tilton, but rather a slap at all who believe in the foolishness of fundamentalist/pentecostal Christianity. All Bible-believing Christians were held up to ridicule by "Prime Time Live." All such Christians were disdained by ABC as simple-minded suckers.

The Texas attorney general who brought suit against Tilton was taken in as well. He initiated his suit under pressure from constituents who had watched the television special. But the injunction he sought against Word of Faith was denied by the judge who heard it. In fact, the judge censured the attorney general. He said the attorney general's action was "neither professional nor responsible, bordering on the unethical and constitutes, 'bad faith.'"[2] The judge went so far as to say the attorney general had dishonored "his lawyers, his office, his profession, the courts, and the citizens of the state of Texas, who he was elected to support."[3]

The fact that "Prime Time" was unscrupulous in its attack on Tilton, Grant, and Lea does not mean that the preachers are without sin. It does not mean that everything they have done in their ministries is beyond reproach, or that it always comes up to the biblical level of responsibility and accountability. But that is not the point. The point is that if a man is to be hanged, it should be for a crime he has actually committed. It is not enough to simply say Robert Tilton is a bad guy. In America the Bill of Rights guarantees all of us a fair trial—even those of us some people view as ridiculous. Robert Tilton, by the way, has sued Diane Sawyer and ABC News. Tilton's Word of Faith Ministry has responded to the ABC program with a program called "Prime Time Lies."[4]

Christians, of all people, must carefully guard the workings of justice. Christians understand that we are all sinners; we are all guilty in general, and for our guiltiness, God has provided a sacrifice for sin in His Son. On the other hand, God is explicit about the ways in which we bring accusations against people. According to the Bible, condemnation of the guilty needs to be backed up by specific charges and supported by real proof. Civil liberties are held in high esteem in the Western world only because of our Judeo-Christian heritage. God's law in both the Old and New Testaments guarantees that our subjective feelings about the unrighteousness of other people are not enough to condemn them. The guilty are condemned only after they have been "brought to justice" and their guilt established "in the mouth of two or three witnesses." A man's good name is jealously protected by rules of justice in the Bible.

Historically, we have determined that judgment should come through a jury of peers, not at the hands of a hostile press. Tilton, Lea, and Grant were tried on national television by a wholly secular press, a press that makes no bones about the fact that it scorns Bible-thumpers. Ample evidence exists to support the claim that the press feels it has the responsibility to protect the citizens of America from preachers. That knowledge should make Christians slow to accept allegations against Christian ministries, especially when those allegations arise from a biased source.

The Feeding Frenzy Mentality

I, like millions of other Christians who watched the "Prime Time" special, was saddened. Even worse, I believed—almost unquestionably—what I saw. Yes, there was a part of me that recognized that Diane Sawyer and her crew probably were prejudiced, but by the end of the hour the sheer volume of their allegations—and the graphic and convincing ways in which they were presented—added up in my mind to proof. In some ways, I could identify with the publisher of the *Tulsa Christian Times*, who editorialized:

> I bought into the "Prime Time Live" story on Tilton, Grant and Lea. It was easy. I dislike Tilton's preaching and what appears to be his money-grubbing style. It seemed that, like Jim Bakker, he was now getting his "just desserts."

> Then information started trickling in that disturbed me. Piece by piece, the parts began to fit together that suggested "Prime Time Live" had grossly misused their powerful journalistic position. . .[5]

What accounts for our willingness to receive public accusations against brothers? Perhaps one reason is that we have become accustomed to seeing influential people brought to ruin by a hostile press. Larry J. Sabato speaks to this issue in his book, *Feeding Frenzy: How Attack Journalism Has Transformed American Politics*:

> It has become a spectacle without equal in modern American politics: the news media, print and broad-

cast, go after a wounded politician like sharks in a
feeding frenzy. The wounds may have been self-in-
flicted, and the politician may richly deserve his or
her fate, but the journalists now take center stage in
the process, creating the news as much as reporting
it. . . .[6]

Sabato provides us with a picturesque description of
a feeding frenzy:

In the animal world, no activity is more classically
frenzied than the feeding of sharks, piranhas, or blue-
fish when they encounter a wounded prey. These
attack-fish with extraordinarily acute senses first search
out weak, ill, or injured targets. On locating them,
each hunter moves in quickly to gain a share of the
kill, feeding not just off the victim but also off its
fellow hunters' agitation. The excitement and drama
of the violent encounter builds to a crescendo, sometimes overwhelming the creatures' usual inhibitions.
The frenzy can spread, with the delirious attackers
wildly striking any object that moves in the water,
even each other.[7]

The amazing phenomena of the feeding frenzy is this:
Although we know it is happening, we are continually
taken in by it and even participate in it. It is not that we
are gullible. Most of us recognize the feeding frenzy happening around us and condemn it. Why then are we
unable to resist the temptation to be drawn into the fray?
Is the smell of blood simply too tempting to resist? Probably a better answer is that we are so inundated by the
process that we are unable to extract ourselves from it.
The feeding frenzy has affected our ability to be objective
observers and just jurors. But it is worse and goes deeper
than that. It is part of a recent change in our social and
psychological makeup.

The feeding frenzy pattern is part of a foundational
change in modern communication. This rapid and widespread revolution affects the way we process information
and what we believe is true. The change has been so
subtle that we have been unaware that it has been occur-

ring. Dozens of sophisticated alterations in our methods of communication have produced a society in which truth has literally "fallen in the street" (Is. 59:14).

This basic change—a change that affects everything—is that we have become a people who come to truth by propaganda rather than by reason.

The Feeding Frenzy Accompanies the Fall of Reason

Our basic problem is that we have stopped thinking clearly. We no longer know how to arrive at truth.

For at least the past twenty years, numerous godly prophets have accurately portrayed the decline in moral judgment in America. Men like Charles Colson and the late Frances Schaeffer have adequately documented the passing of America into the post-Christian (really post-theistic) age. Other Christian commentators point to the rise of easy divorce, homosexuality, and pornography, along with a host of other sins, as milestones marking our decline.

Secular observers also lament the decline of American culture. They suggest the reason for the decline is that we have abandoned the wisdom that has made us great. The decline in moral virtue is attributed by them to a neutralizing of our value system. At the heart of the problem is the modern philosophy of *moral relativism*, the concept that all ideas are as good as all others, that nothing is either absolutely right or absolutely wrong. The late Dr. Allan Bloom lamented our decent into moral relativism when he wrote that freshmen who enter college in this modern age have one thing in common—their relativism.

> There is one thing a professor can be absolutely certain of: almost every student entering the university believes, or says he believes, that truth is relative. . . some are religious, some atheists; some are to the Left, some to the Right; some intend to be scientists, some humanists or professionals or businessmen; some are poor, some rich. They are unified only in their relativism. . . the danger they have been taught to fear is not error but intolerance. . . the true believer is the real danger.[8]

Moral relativism is flawed thinking, wrong thinking. When, for example, we wrote laws against polygamy, adultery, and fornication, we did so not to infringe upon individual liberty, but to protect society. Fidelity in marriage is the glue that holds together the family—the primary unit of society. Promiscuous sex destroys families. "Free love" is a philosophical mistake; it is an oxymoron. Love is not free nor cheap but very costly; it is maintained only at great sacrifice. Every historian knows that great societies have always fallen when they became self-indulgent, sexually excessive, and interested only in entertainment (the "bread and circuses" of Rome).

Moral relativism eventually results in foolishness. When we abandon the belief that some ideas are superior to others, we are left to honor all values, cultures, and behaviors as equal. This leads us to accept inane ideas as valuable. For example, we allow women to abort their fetuses at will because we have decided that the fetus is not human but simply tissue. The baby's fate, we have told ourselves, rests in the hands of the mother carrying it because, "she must have control over her own body."

A San Diego court recently convicted twenty-one-year-old Robert Anthony Davis of first-degree murder when he shot a pregnant woman. The woman survived, but the fetus aborted.[9] The dilemma is that the fetus, whether wanted or unwanted by the mother, must either be a human being or merely tissue—it can't be both. If it is human, we are correct in bringing murder charges against Davis, but we need to extend those charges to every woman who aborts her fetus. If, on the other hand, the fetus is only tissue, we cannot prosecute Davis for murder. We might prosecute him for assaulting the mother, but we can't accuse him of murdering tissue.

The basic disrespect for reason and logic means truth is no longer a matter of reason, but a function of propaganda! Truth in such a society winds up being determined by the organization that can mount the best ad campaign, enlist enough supporters, and declare itself the winner in the debate. Whether or not its position is right is secondary.

This sloppy, irrational disrespect for reasoned truth has driven secular journalism for thirty years. It is now being emulated by the heresy hunters.

The Fall of Reason Results from Abandoning the Word of God

Moral decline results from disobedience to the Word of God. When God made the world and set man in it, He immediately gave him life-and-death information. God gave laws so we could find life. His Word was written first on stone tablets, then on scrolls, and finally in the Bible. Western civilization rose to supremacy upon the foundation of the Judeo-Christian law. The English Revolution and Parliament resulted from the broad publication of the Bible in English. The American Revolution and Constitution, along with all Western democracies, trace their rule to the moral precepts and human rights extolled in scripture.

The foolishness of moral relativism has even breached the walls of the Church. For the past two years, the prestigious Presbyterian Church (USA) has toyed with advocating extremely liberal views on sexual conduct. Its Committee on Sexuality has sent to the floor of the General Assembly resolutions that say:

> There is no single, consistent biblical ethic of sexuality. The Church should "repent" of its oppressive morality, which is the work of white patriarchal "heterosexists." It urges the church not to "restrict sexual activity to marriage alone," but to celebrate all forms of sexual intimacy, "marital, premarital or post marital." It states celibacy should no longer be the "only moral option for single persons."

> Regarding teen-agers and sex, it advises youngsters to make decisions on the basis of "mutuality," "consent," and "maturity." The report omits any mention of the Seventh Commandment—"Thou Shalt Not Commit Adultery."[10]

Meanwhile, Episcopalians have considered a proposal that their denomination should endorse the view that homosexuality is a "God-given" state and that gay relationships are "holy, life-giving and grace-filled."[11] Methodists pondered a report claiming that the New Testament injunctions against homosexuality were really aimed only at the homosexual abuse of children (pederasty) and homosexual acts by people who were "naturally heterosexual." Paul, the argument goes, would have been more understanding if he knew as much about human sexual variance as modern society does.[12] Such foggy thinking within the church leadership shows up in the rank and file of the Church. In a recent opinion poll of people who say they worship regularly, only 39 percent said, "It's always wrong for an unmarried adult to have sex," and only 65 percent said, "It's always wrong for an unmarried teen-ager to have sex." Surely, "A mist in the pulpit is a fog in the pew."

The Fall of Reason is a Fall from the Written Word

The fall of moral virtue and the ascendancy of moral relativism is, therefore, a fall from the Word of God. However the decline in respect for the Word of God is not merely a result of our rebellion to the rule of God; to some degree, it results from our inability to understand the Word of God. That is the point of this chapter: the feeding frenzy (truth by propaganda instead of reason) occurs not only because we have abandoned God, but because we have abandoned reason. This abandonment allows the heresy hunters to strike out in unreasonable ways against Christian ministries who are "different." The heresy hunters are often unable to understand that being different is not the same as being wrong. Again, a cause of our abandonment of reason is that we no longer communicate primarily by words but rather by images. Images, slogans, and snippets of out-of-context information are grist for the propaganda mills, but they are the death of reason.

Neil Postman wrote the book, *Amusing Ourselves to Death*. In it he says:

The most significant American cultural fact of the
second half of the twentieth century (is) the decline
of the Age of Typography and the ascendancy of the
Age of Television. This change-over has dramatically
and irreversibly shifted the content and meaning of
public discourse. . . [13]

Postman says we have "trivialized" communication.
He maintains it is impossible to convey important and
complex ideas through a medium that relies almost entirely upon thirty-second sound bites. He goes so far as to
say "much of our public discourse has become dangerous
nonsense."

The warning about the threat of popular media to
logical thinking has been sounded for decades. Marshall
McLuhan, the Canadian educator, said, "The medium is
the message." He meant that the way we communicate
ideas determines what we are able to communicate.
McLuhan specifically meant that the television age—or the
age of electronic media—limits the way we are able to
communicate.

The upshot of the comments of McLuhan, Postman,
and others is that we have turned from reason and logic
to propaganda. We have begun to rely more on pictures
and attitudes for communication than upon words and
reasons.

Trivial Pursuits

When Neil Postman says modern communication has
been "trivialized," he means that when we abandoned the
rigorous debate of evidence, we reduced truth to propaganda and opinion. We "come down" on one side or
another of an issue. We have an opinion and are little
interested in hearing its arguments. Heresy hunters jump
to conclusions: "No one," they say, "with a bouffant hair
style, who wears sharkskin suits, and blows on people so
they are 'slain in the spirit' can be a man of God!" Likewise, a man like Kenneth Copeland, who believes Christians can "take authority over their finances," must be "in
it for the money." And Bob Larson's constant shouting at

the devil during his radio show, his relentless appeals for money, and his belief that children are being sacrificed by Satanists characterize a man who is either insincere or irrational. Finally, Mike Warnke (a pudgy Christian comedian no less!) also believes in satanic conspiracy theories. And his marital instability, the heresy hunters decide, is proof that his theology on Satanism is wrong and that he doubtless fabricated his testimony of involvement in the occult.

I contend that the new breed of Christian media people—the heresy hunters—have been over-influenced by the world. Many are undeniably Christians, but as journalists they are secularized. They have fallen into the feeding frenzy mentality. Flimsy allegations and suspicions excite them in the same way the smell of blood excites sharks. Once they "determine" that a ministry needs to be taken out, they abandon reason (and very often scripture) and set about to bring down the Christian ministers they judge to be unworthy.

"Christian" Attack Journalism?

Men like Benny Hinn, Larry Lea, and Robert Tilton not only minister to thousands on television but they also each pastor churches of several thousand people and have led thousands of people to the Lord. Surely they deserve better than the treatment they have received at the hands of the heresy hunters.

The list of those so maligned in print and over the airwaves also includes others who deserve better.

In November of 1992, *Christianity Today* reported that "nearly three dozen" cult-watch organizations were branding as heresy the Resurrection teaching of Dr. Murray Harris, professor of New Testament exegesis and theology at Trinity Evangelical Divinity School. These watchdog groups, led by Witness, Inc., contended that Harris teaches doctrine similar to that of Jehovah's Witnesses.[14] According to the president of Trinity, Harris has been evaluated by an august committee made up of theologians from Southwest Baptist Theological Seminary,

Denver Conservative Baptist Seminary, and Reformed Theological Seminary. They pronounced him "within the bounds of orthodoxy."[15]

None of that stopped the cult-watchers. In March of 1993, Witness Inc. mailed out a "special update" on the controversy. They referred to the efforts of the committee as a "type of kangaroo court."[16] They have circulated a form letter condemning Harris' doctrine, appealing for Christians to sign it and return it to them.

My point is that Harris needs to be treated better than he has been by those who set themselves up to be guardians of the Church. Obviously, disagreement exists over Harris' opinions. However, until such time as he is clearly judged heretical, it strikes me as unreasonable to mount a huge public relations campaign against him.

To a lesser extent, men like Jack Hayford, John Wimber, Oral Roberts, Pat Robertson, Paul Crouch, Jack Van Impe, Jack Hyles, and Tony Campolo have been subjected to innuendo and "suggestion." The feeding frenzy mentality reaches to every level of the Church. In most of the cases the charges were ill-founded, exaggerated, or completely without basis. Nevertheless, like feathers shaken into the wind, they blow around forever.

Christian ministers expect the secular press to despise them, but they are always shocked when they are counted unworthy by their brothers. Neither Billy Sunday nor Oral Roberts expected the secular world to understand them or like them. That is enemy fire. But friendly fire is a different matter. When heresy hunters function as secular attack journalists, such casualties are sure to occur. My hope is that we can limit such losses.

I maintain that Christian "attack journalism" is neither fair nor biblical. In some cases it results from simple ignorance, from people who find themselves in positions of influence beyond their wisdom. Giving a printing press to the immature is like handing a loaded revolver to a child. In other cases the ungodliness stems from root problems such as pride and bitterness. In all cases where ministers attack other ministers with abandon and without regard to scripture, indiscretion reigns.

In the following chapters I will examine specific cases where I think heresy hunters have abandoned the rule of reason and scripture to participate in the ungodly feeding frenzy which has been such a detriment to the Body of Christ.

CHAPTER 3

In Search of Heresy

Apparently, Benny Hinn turns a lot of people off; his style bothers many Christians. It seems some folks don't like his bouffant hairdo, his flashy clothes, his authoritative manner of speaking, and particularly, his showmanship. "He blows on people and they fall down!" his detractors say. "How can that be godly?" Hinn also is given to saying (in his own words) "dumb" things in the heat of sermonizing, which he later wishes he hadn't said.

I heard about Hinn long before I ever watched him preach. Eventually I saw him on TV in Arizona. From the things I had heard about him, I doubted I would like him. And, in fact, I was initially put off by his style. However, I was surprised to find his sermon (actually more of a testimony) to be both entertaining and inspiring.

About a year after I had first seen Benny Hinn on TV, a pastor in Roseburg, Oregon, asked me if I had read Hinn's new, controversial book, *Good Morning Holy Spirit*. Someone had told the pastor the book was heretical, and he wanted to know my opinion. I immediately bought it, read it, and then wrote to the pastor and said the book, in my opinion, was not heretical. Hinn was less precise in his theology than I would have liked, but I did not think the book was meant to be a theological treatise. It was a testimony, and I thought it was a powerful one.

Not everyone agrees with my assessment of Hinn's book or of his ministry. In fact, many popular apologists

have come out against the book and the work of Benny
Hinn. Hank Hanegraaff, who succeeded Dr. Walter Martin as head of the Christian Research Institute (CRI), is
one of those who believes Hinn teaches heresy in *Good
Morning Holy Spirit*. Hanegraaff circulated a position pa
per calling some of Hinn's statements "blatantly false
and some of his teachings "blatantly blasphemous." In
published statement on Hinn's ministry, Hanegraaff sai
"Hinn's so-called revelations could not have come fro
the Lord. One is left to wonder what 'spirit' Hinn is
listening to and led by."[1]

On the radio show "The Bible Answer Man,"
Hanegraaff rejected Hinn's claim that he receives teaching from the Holy Spirit. Commenting on what Hanegraaff
thought was a particularly ludicrous "revelation," he said,
"Benny Hinn's Holy Spirit is a worse buffoon than Benny
is!"[2]

No one can deny that Hinn makes outlandish statements. For example, he once taught that Adam, before
the Fall, could fly. He also once preached that God origi-
nally designed women to give birth out of their sides.
(Later, when asked about the statement, he admitted that
it was a "dumb" thing to say.)[3] Hinn has acknowledged
that much of the misunderstanding about his ministry is
his own fault. He blames it partly on his lack of formal
Bible training and says, "The Lord launched me into
ministry almost overnight."[4]

So is Hinn a heretic? At what point does a preacher
deserve to be branded in that way? How many dumb
statements makes someone a heretic? If an otherwise
orthodox preacher makes a doctrinal mistake, is he a
heretic? More to the point, who decides? These are questions that require thoughtful answers, not snap judgments.
Before we look at the specific charges against Hinn or
others currently branded as heretical, we need to discuss
the definition of the term *heresy*.

Who Are the Heretics?

One of the first things you discover when searching for a precise definition of the word *heresy* is that no commonly accepted definition exists. The word is used only a very few times in the Bible, and the original meaning of the word was not particularly negative. It simply expressed the idea of "choosing." Matthew employs the Greek word for heresy when he writes of the beginning of Jesus' earthly ministry. In describing the miracles attesting to Jesus' anointing he says (quoting Isaiah), "Behold my servant, whom I have *chosen*; my beloved, in whom my soul is well pleased: I will put my spirit upon him, and he shall show judgment to the Gentiles" (Matt. 12:18).

Heresy often simply meant a chosen party or position. Pharisees, Sadducees, and Essenes were parties or sects within Judaism. Although these parties took very different positions on many issues, they saw each other as parts of the one nation of Israel—God's chosen people. In the early years of the Church, while Christianity was beginning to emerge out of Judaism, new believers in Christ often remained in one of its sects. It was not yet clear that Christianity was to be a distinct religion from Judaism: "Then some of the believers who belonged to the party [literally *heresy*] of the Pharisees stood up and said, 'The Gentiles must be circumcised and required to obey the law of Moses'" (Acts 15:5 NIV).

Nevertheless, before the close of the New Testament, the term heresy began to define division within the Church, not simply diversity. By the end of the ministry of the Apostle Paul, the Jewish majority was calling the sect of Nazarenes a "heresy" or "party" in a way that clearly indicated that they saw Christianity as a separate and wrong sect. When Paul was brought before the Judean governor, Felix, for trial, the charge was religious sedition: "For we have found this man a pestilent fellow, and a mover of sedition among all the Jews throughout the world, and a ringleader of the sect [literally heresy] of the Nazarenes" (Acts 24:5).

Paul, however, denied he was a heretic. In his defense he said, "They cannot prove the things they accuse me of. But this I confess unto thee, that after the way which they call heresy, so worship I the God of my fathers, believing all things which are written in the law and in the prophets: And have hope toward God, which they themselves also allow, that there shall be a resurrection of the dead, both of the just and unjust" (Acts 24:14-15).

The Essence of Heresy

Heresy came to describe ideas that were so different that they struck at the basic unity of the Body of Christ. In the early centuries A.D., heretics were those who professed those destructive spiritual ideas. The early councils of the Church met to decide which ideas were so far wrong as to be considered damning. Those great councils hammered out definitions that have stood the test of time.

The early councils of the Church and their definitions of such important doctrines as the Trinity continue to guide us today, as yardsticks by which we can judge novel theology. But still, theologians understand that spiritual truth is often elusive. Christians throughout history have recognized that it is impossible to know a man's heart simply by listening to his recitation of a catechism; some wonderful Christians have very primitive theology. On the other hand, some great theologians are far from having a personal relationship with Jesus. They know about Him, but they don't know Him.

One concept continues to surface in any search for a definition of heresy; heretical ideas destroy the Church by dividing it. Division is the fruit of heresy.

We can't underestimate the seriousness of division. According to the Bible, one of our first duties as members of the Body of Christ is to understand that our relationship is not only with Jesus but also with other Christians. Our fellowship within the Church is often called our communion. With time we understand that our communion is not only the joyous fruit of our salvation, but that it is also the vital force that ensures the ongoing health of the Body of Christ. Our loving communion enlarges and perpetuates the Body by displaying Christ to the unsaved. It is how they know we are Christians (John 13:34-35).

Essential to our communion is that we must have the ability to recognize our brothers and sisters in Christ, to be able to "discern the Lord's body" (1 Cor. 11:29-30). If we don't, we are in danger of excluding genuine Christians from our communion. In so doing, we strike a devastating blow to the work of God.

Our unity is so important, Jesus' priestly prayer admonishes us to "be one" (John 17:22). Likewise, we not only must recognize the Body of Christ, but we are also charged with preserving it:

> I therefore, the prisoner of the Lord, beseech you that ye walk worthy of the vocation wherewith ye are called, with all lowliness and meekness, with long-suffering, forbearing one another in love; endeavoring to keep the unity of the Spirit in the bond of peace.
>
> There is one body, and one Spirit, even as ye are called in one hope of your calling;
>
> One Lord, one faith, one baptism, One God and Father of all, who is above all, and through all, and in you all. (Eph. 4:1-6)

The Definition of Heresy

The theologian Harold O. J. Brown suggests heresy must have at least two primary components: First, it designates a doctrine or teaching that is clearly wrong. Second, heresy must be an important issue.

Brown, in his book *Heresies*, says:

> In Christian usage the term *heresy* refers to a false doctrine, i.e. one that is simply not true and that is, in addition, so important that those who believe it, whom the church calls heretics, must be considered to have abandoned the faith.[5]

The Source of Heresy

As I wrestle to understand the heresy/heretic controversy, one thing is clear to me—heresy originates with false prophets. The Apostle Peter says it this way:

> For the prophecy came not in old time by the will of man: but holy men of God spake as they were moved by the Holy Ghost.
>
> But there were false prophets also among the people, even as there shall be false teachers among you, who privily shall bring in damnable heresies, even denying the Lord that bought them, and bring upon themselves swift destruction.
>
> And many shall follow their pernicious ways; by reason of whom the way of truth shall be evil spoken of. (2 Pet. 1:21–2:2)

Paul says something similar when he tells us that false brethren have an agenda:

> For I know this, that after my departing shall grievous wolves enter in among you, not sparing the flock.
>
> Also of your own selves shall men arise, speaking perverse things, to draw away disciples after them. (Acts 20:29-30)

False prophets introduce bad ideas into the Church because they are. . . false prophets. Something in their carnal nature not only refuses to submit to the law of God but also invents foolishness in its place. The source of heresy is rebellion to God.

We get another look at this aspect of heresy from the Apostle John. Writing in the fourth chapter of 1 John (verses 1-6), he describes the relationship between what he calls "the spirit of antichrist" and the doctrine produced by it. The antichrist spirit, he says, always produces a refusal to confess that Jesus Christ has come in the flesh. This false teaching derives from a stubbornness. Without discussing the exact meaning of this doctrine (or confession), we need to see that there is a vital connection between the spirit and the confession. John suggests that this ungodliness comes from false prophets that "have gone out into the world."

Further, in the second chapter of the same book, John identifies the source from which these false prophets come. He also reveals their essential nature:

> Little children, it is the last time: and as ye have heard that antichrist shall come, even now are there many antichrists; whereby we know that it is the last time. They went out from us, but they were not of us; for if they had been of us, they would no doubt have continued with us: but they went out, that they might be made manifest that they were not all of us. (1 John 2:18-19)

Heresy consists of these two elements, heresy and the heretic, that pursue each other in circular orbits. Genuine heretics possessed of bad hearts devise damnable heresies. These bad ideas in turn destroy the faith of some or at least prevent them from coming to wholesome faith. In the second generation, those infected with the bad teaching pass it on to others.

While I believe the healthy Church has the responsibility to seek out, challenge, and expose both heretics and heresy, it is at this point that the heresy hunters miss a vital truth: *While all heretical doctrine needs to be destroyed, not all those who bear that doctrine do.* This is a subtle point and easily missed. It simply means that when we discover people possessed of a heretical doctrine, we must not conclude that they are irreconcilable heretics.

What will better guide the sincere heresy hunters is the notion that they need to hunt the heresy, not the heretic. If the genuine apologist remembers that his primary job is to restore all men, both to bring the unsaved to life in Christ and to bring the erring brother back into the fold, he will be a better servant of the Lord. This approach will allow him to consider that the man who speaks heresy may not yet be totally divided from the Body. It is sometimes true that those who repeat heresy have not yet been perverted by it. Sometimes they can be turned:

> Brethren, if any of you do err from the truth, and one
> convert him; let him know, that he which converteth
> the sinner from the error of his way shall save a soul
> from death, and shall hide a multitude of sins. (James
> 5:19-20)

Differentiating between Heresy and Heretic

In addition to being unclear about the real nature of
heresy, the heresy hunters often mix up the man and his
message. The wisest counselors in the Church have always
tried to differentiate between the heretic and his heresy.
They have been slow to speak out against the heretic,
even when they were quick and incisive in condemning
the heresy. St. Augustine displayed this attitude when he
dealt with the ancient Pelagian heresy. Pelagius was a
British monk who thought it was possible to live without
sin. Augustine, on the other hand, thought such an idea
was destructive. It undermined, he said, "all that the
Apostle taught about the sinful nature of man." These
men, Augustine said, "have no idea of the depth of the
corrupt nature of sinful flesh!" However, Augustine never
mentioned Pelagius' name. Later, in recounting the battle,
he gave his reasons:

> I refrained from inserting Pelagius' name in my work,
> wherein I refuted this book of his; for I thought I
> should render a prompter assistance to the truth if I
> continued to preserve a friendly relation to him, and
> so to spare his personal feelings, while at the same
> time I showed no mercy, as I bound not to show it,
> to the productions of his pen.[6]

I am not, I wish to add, making the case that apologists should never "name names." I am more interested in
the attitude of the argument and the motive of the attack.
The attitude must be reasonable; the motive must be to
restore, where possible, the erring brother. History tells
us that when men of God have serious differences, they
will best serve the Church if they find a way to talk about
the problems in good faith.

Differentiating between Heresy and Sin

Heresy hunters not only have difficulty differentiating between heresy and heretics, they also confuse heresy with sin. All heresy is sin, but not all sin is heresy. Some of the charges against the "heretics," such as sexual misconduct or mismanagement of ministry funds, are really questions of ethics, not doctrine.

Don't misunderstand me. We certainly have a right and duty to challenge the ethics, as well as the doctrines, of Christian ministers. But the differences in the two charges suggest that the way to deal with them may be different. Of course, all the same biblical rules for confronting Christian brothers still apply in both cases; we must approach them humbly, lovingly, patiently, and within the framework of the scriptural mandate.

One of the differences between personal sin and the sin of preaching doctrinal error is obvious. Doctrinal sin can be addressed without dealing directly with the sinner, but moral failure cannot. Apologists can deal with error within, say, the hyper-faith movement without maligning or making a personal attack on those who teach it. However, moral failure such as sexual sin must be addressed directly to the sinner.

It is essential, I think, to understand that apologists are not necessarily pastors. An apologist speaks to doctrinal errors, a pastor speaks to personal and moral errors. It is possible to deal with theory and theology in cold, clinical analysis, but effective personal correction can only flow through the gates of a loving relationship.

Can a Man Teach Heresy and Not Be a Heretic?

By defining heresy as that which arises from the rebellious spirit of a heretic, we may be able to better distinguish between real heretics and their victims. A person who ignorantly reports heretical ideas is wrong, but he may not be properly called a heretic.

I observe this phenomenon as I minister to the cults. Perhaps I am able to be patient with Mormons because I am a former Mormon Elder myself. I was married in the

Mormon temple and served faithfully in nearly every
auxiliary of the Mormon Church. I remember that as a
Mormon I loved God and wanted with all my heart to
serve Him. But I was wrong about the way in which He
required me to serve Him. My doctrine was wrong; my
theology was wrong; my methods were wrong. In short, I
was a heretic by all definitions of doctrine.

Because of my own experience, when I minister to
Latter-day Saints, I do not see them as heretics. I see them
as victims of heresy. When I talk to a Mormon Bishop
who is trying, in the best way he knows, to serve God, I
am moved with compassion towards him. I realize his
error not only may cost him his eternal soul, but it costs
him in a thousand other ways every day of his life. Should
we not see the heretic with compassion?

When I do challenge Mormonism, I challenge the
doctrines, not the people. I never say, "You are a heretic!
You are leading people to hell!" If we are compassionate
with those who bring such a grievous error, should we not
also be compassionate with Benny Hinn, Robert Tilton,
Kenneth Copeland, and Mike Warnke? That is the point
of this book.

It is also important to remember that the theology of
the Christian ministers currently under attack by the heresy hunters has not been proven to be as grievously wrong
as Mormon doctrine. A few heresy hunters say, "If we
don't excommunicate Kenneth Copeland, we owe an
apology to Joseph Smith (the founder of Mormonism)."
Not so! Mormonism is wrong in so many important ways
that the best minds of Bible-centered Christianity have
declared its doctrine heretical. Copeland et al. are under
attack by heresy hunters who want to demonstrate that
those men are heretics. I do not believe they have yet
demonstrated it. The Church at large has made a broad-
based, reluctant, and solemn declaration that Mormonism
is heretical. That is not the same as the passionate declaration of a group of self-appointed heresy hunters about
Hinn and others.

The Balance: Truth and Love

Apologists who do not guard themselves can become excessively suspicious. Benny Hinn is a colorful but effective minister of the gospel. The charges against him do not add up to heresy. His enemies don't like his "packaging" or style. The heresy hunters have wronged him.

The work of the apologist is a noble one, but it is difficult and fraught with many dangers. The greatest danger of all is that those who presume to deal with such heady concepts may, themselves, wind up dividing the Church. In that tragic case, ironically, they become the real heretics.

Sometimes men become overimpressed with their role as watchdogs in the Church. At other times they simply have zeal without wisdom. Still others are jealous of other ministries. Sometimes they are prejudiced against certain styles of ministry. They forget our common frailty, sin, and selfishness. In striking off the offending hand, they are destroying their own bodies.

They need to be very careful in their judgment. They cannot allow their prejudices to direct their criticism. They must learn to judge, "not according to appearance, but to judge righteous judgment" (John 7:24).

CHAPTER 4

Sins of Prejudice

Heresy hunters leveled charges of heresy against Benny Hinn shortly after the publication of his first book, *Good Morning Holy Spirit* (Thomas Nelson Publishers, 1990). This book immediately went to the top of the Christian best-seller list and stayed there, according to *Publishers Weekly* magazine, "week after week, month after month." It has now sold nearly a million copies.

Although Hinn is pastor of the megachurch, Orlando Christian Center, in Orlando, according to *Christianity Today* magazine, he was virtually unknown outside charismatic circles until the book's publication. *Good Morning Holy Spirit* is Hinn's testimony of his conversion and unique experience with God. Even Hinn's critics are forced to admit the purpose of the book is to call people to live a Spirit-filled life. However, it also attempts to explain Hinn's understanding of who God is and how He manifests Himself to us. It is within that explanation that some of the charges of heresy arise. One reviewer found what he described as "implicit" heresy in the book.

Hinn has also been labeled a "Faith Teacher." (We will take up the issue of the so-called "Faith Message" in chapter 7). Christian Research Institute's Hank Hanegraaff says the Faith Teachers are unquestionably heretics. On "The Bible Answer Man" radio show Hanegraaff said:

> I have to tell you I have to sit here and read the letters
> of those who are not only dying—but have died—as a
> direct result of the teaching of Mr. Copeland, Mr.
> Hinn, Marilyn Hickey, and a host of other perverted
> teachers on the Trinity Broadcasting Network.[1]

Another cult-watch organization, Personal Freedom Outreach (PFO), has featured at least two exposés of Hinn:

> Time and again preachers burst onto the scene, at-
> tracting attention and followers with what they claim
> are new insights into scripture and new powers from
> God, only to be exposed as being not only unoriginal
> but false. . . his message is not to be trusted. His
> methods are borrowed. His spiritual gift—"his anoint-
> ing"—is counterfeit.[2]

PFO's newsletter says *Good Morning Holy Spirit* contains "gross theological errors."

Many other Christians, however, are equally vocal in their defense of Hinn. He is a regular visitor on Trinity Broadcasting Network's "Praise The Lord Show" where he and the host, Paul Crouch, have said the real problem lies not with Hinn, but with his attackers. If you listen to CRI's "The Bible Answer Man," you will hear dozens of callers voice their love and support for Hinn. Hanegraaff recently reported Hinn was the "number one topic" on the show.

In fact, Hinn's most studious critics refuse to label *Good Morning Holy Spirit* clearly heretical. Robert Bowman, a former staff member at CRI, wrote a book review of *Good Morning Holy Spirit* for the *Christian Research Journal*. The review, "A Summary Critique," suggests the book is dangerous but not "explicitly" heretical. Instead, Bowman calls it "implicitly tritheistic." Implicit tritheism, I suggest, is a little esoteric and certainly cannot be sufficient grounds for CRI's continued charge of heresy against Hinn. That Bowman does not consider the book clearly heretical is demonstrated by his comments in the review:

There is much about what Benny Hinn says concerning the Trinity with which orthodox Christians can agree. Hinn affirms that God is a "triune being" and that the three persons "are really one in Being" (70, 71, 74). He states clearly that the Father, Son and Holy Spirit are each fully God, emphasizing that the Holy Spirit is just as much God as the Father and the Son (69-71, 87, 90, 131). He also insists that the Holy Spirit is just as real and personal as the Father and Son (2, 51, 71). As God, third person of the Trinity (49, 73), the Holy Spirit is omnipresent (73, 87-88), unlike the angels or the Devil (88), and he is also omnipotent and omniscient (88-89). The Holy Spirit is a personal friend, companion, and counselor to the Christian (52).[3]

In a personal letter to me, Bowman said, "I would have to agree [with you] that the book contained no statement which indisputably must be regarded as 'heresy.'" Likewise, *Christianity Today* asked the charismatic theologian J. Rodman Williams, a professor at Regent University, to examine Hinn's teachings. Williams said he found *Good Morning Holy Spirit* "very profitable." However, Williams said Hinn has made some "theologically erroneous statements."[4] In spite of those errors and what Williams perceives to be other ministry flaws, he told *Christianity Today* that Hinn "is a man God is using today." And, he said, many people have been blessed by his ministry.[5]

The Nature of the Charges

Charges against Hinn have avalanched since the release of *Good Morning Holy Spirit*. After the initial challenge to his doctrine, the attack shifted to his ministry style and his claim to "anointing." Personal Freedom Outreach is typical of many of Hinn's critics when it publishes—apparently as an example of Hinn's gross theological error—the following statement:

Hinn claims his "anointing" has given him supernatural powers. He says that he hears directly from God—in one account through a radio not tuned to a sta-

tion!—and that he can knock people off their feet
without touching them.[6]

These claims indeed make Hinn sound strange. Those
who receive such out-of-context information about him
are sure to think he is an oddball. We picture a weird
evangelist who "hears voices" and who walks up to strang-
ers and says, "Hey, I can knock you off your feet without
touching you!" Nothing could be further from the real
Benny Hinn.

Part of the problem, I sincerely believe, is that well-
meaning heresy hunters are prejudiced by their own personal Christian experience. They are turned off by things
they don't understand and have not experienced. I certainly know how that can happen. We can be very uncom-
fortable about the worship experiences of others. I admit
I am not at all comfortable around so-called "high-church"
services. Being an Evangelical, I am uneasy with pageantry,
gilded altars, incense, and formal liturgy. But though they
are strange to me, that does not make them necessarily
wrong—certainly not heretical. On the other hand, my
personal Christian experience and background allow me
to tolerate many things that other mature Christians who
haven't had my experience can't stomach. I can give preachers a break who raise their voices, turn red in the face,
and get excited when they preach. I, with Abraham Lincoln, enjoy a preacher who looks as if "he is fighting a
swarm of bees." True, some excesses in histrionics turn
me off, but they are not so strange to me that I discount
the accompanying message. Likewise, I am able to listen
for and appreciate a message in a sermon delivered by a
man who is uneducated and rough. In fact, I'd rather hear
a crude sermon with content than a polished, empty one.

But not everyone is happy with the meat of the gospel
served up like a Big Mac; they prefer their fare with
candlelight or at least with a clean tablecloth. For that
reason, many of the heresy hunters are very uncomfort-
able with the Pentecostal environment. To some it seems
to be a whole genre of sermonizing and worship that is
distasteful. I can remember discussing these differences

with a friend who complained, "The trouble with Pentecostal meetings is that they wear me out. I don't like to
stand for an hour while they sing the same choruses over
and over. I got it the first time!" For my part, I explained
that what I didn't like about many non-charismatic services was the tendency to sing "the first and last verse"—
something which makes no sense and seems dry to me.

Many times people are simply reacting to "packaging." They confuse style with content; they mistake form
for doctrine. Over and over Christians have said to me
the reason they don't like Benny Hinn is that "he blows
on people and they fall down!" Or worse, "He throws his
coat at them and they fall down!" They are, of course,
reacting to the charismatic phenomenon of "being slain
in the Spirit." It is a phenomenon akin to "swooning" or
falling into a semi-faint during prayer. It is something that
is common not only to Hinn's ministry but to that of
hundreds of other lesser-known ministers. It is a phenomenon not of the 1990s alone but of the history of the
Church.

Our reaction to such things, however, does not determine the legitimacy of them. Our subjective reaction is
not a reliable guide for our theology. Spiritual experience
does not derive its authenticity from how anybody feels
about it. People can find God in "high-church" worship
whether I like it or not; they can also experience God in
rude tent services fraught with raw emotional experience.
Likewise, whether or not the phenomenon of "being slain
in the Spirit" is legitimate is not a matter of taste. If it is
an act of God's Spirit, then we must be very careful that
we do not assign it to some other source.

The PFO article demonstrates what can happen when
we let our prejudices drive our journalism. When the
authors assert that Hinn claims to hear God through a
radio not tuned to a station, they—in my opinion, are
guilty of ignorance, prejudice, or plain fraud. Their asser-
tion comes from a passage in Hinn's book, *The Anointing*,
in which Hinn attempts to describe some of the providen-

tial dealings of God in his life. He relates how after one very powerful meeting he went to bed and reflected on the meeting:

> "What did you do tonight, Lord?" I asked into the darkness.
>
> Unexpectedly I heard a quick answer: "Be faithful." That was all. "Be faithful."
>
> The next morning I turned on the radio shortly after waking, following my habit of listening to church services as I got ready to go to church myself. The first thing I heard—and I don't have any clue as to the speaker—was: "Watch what you do with the power you have." Then the program instantly went off the air. I can't explain it. I had turned on the radio, a voice had said, "Watch what you do with the power you have," and the voice was gone. I couldn't find it again as I fiddled with the dials.[7]

Now, this account could be described as hearing God's voice through a radio not tuned to a station. What Hinn really said, however, was that the first thing he heard upon turning on the radio, was a preacher saying words which had providential meaning to him, words which confirmed a previous night's spiritual meditation. I venture to say that many a Christian who is submitting his life to God has experienced similar providential interaction with God. He may not have heard God through a radio preacher, but if he has never heard a preacher confirm to his heart what God was previously saying to him, I despair that he can hear God at all. To suggest that this kind of experience is somehow unwholesome is to ridicule a man's testimony, and that is a very unwise practice.

But PFO's characterization of the event described in Hinn's book goes beyond disagreeing with the spiritual nature of what happened. It misrepresents the facts of the case when it claims Hinn heard directly from God "through a radio not tuned to a station." This kind of deliberate misrepresentation of facts epitomizes the lack of balance heresy hunters can fall into in an attempt to make their point. Such activity is not sober evaluation, nor is it apologetics. It is prejudicial heresy hunting. It is a sin of prejudice.

The Danger of Out-of-Context Statements

It is interesting to watch the snowball effect in Christian journalism. Reaction to Hinn seems to have been triggered by an astonishing statement he made on Saturday morning, 15 October 1990—within a few days of the release of *Good Morning Holy Spirit*. Preaching on Trinity Broadcasting Network (TBN), Hinn dropped what was to become probably his most notorious bombshell. Admittedly, the statement was remarkable and ill-conceived. Here it is:

> God the Father is a Person, God the Son is a Person, and God the Holy Ghost is a Person, but each of Them is a triune Being by Himself. If I can shock you, and maybe I should, there's nine of Them.

That is indeed a shocking statement, and in my opinion, it is wrong. Anyone who heard nothing but that telecast could not be faulted for questioning Benny Hinn's theology. No scripturally submitted Christian can thoughtfully defend that remark if it is viewed outside the context of Hinn's overall theology. Apologists have the right—the duty—to challenge such statements. Nevertheless, we must be able to tell the difference between someone who makes occasional outlandish statements in the heat of oratory and someone who preaches "another gospel."

Heresy hunters delight in quoting out-of-context statements. In doing so they oversimplify the complex process of human communication. I believe the most complex form of communication is preaching. Preaching is different from teaching. It is different from theological lecturing, and it is different from purely doctrinal exhortation. John R. W. Stott says preachers are "suspended between heaven and earth," attempting to bridge spiritual ideas across the stream of carnal resistance. They use all kinds of rhetorical devices to explain larger truths.

One of the biggest complaints I have with the heresy

hunters is their propensity to focus on minute slivers of a preached message. Focusing on irregular words or phrases, they enlarge them and pass them around in the Church like candid, uncomplimentary photographs.

Some would suggest that Hinn is not being quoted out of context. I disagree. Context is larger than what the heresy hunters seem to think. Although they are fond of stressing "context" when a cultist wants to excise a sliver of scripture and assign a non-biblical meaning to it, they fail to practice what they preach when it comes to people like Hinn.

Heresy hunters will agree that a word derives its meaning from its context, from how it is used in a sentence. I can illustrate that with an example from our family life. At one time we had a diabetic cat. We had to give him an insulin shot each day. One day I came home to find a note from my wife. It simply said, "Shoot the cat." I knew she meant that she had left without giving him his insulin. I would have been guilty of deliberate misunderstanding if I had executed the cat with a gun.

Cults use out-of-context scripture to undergird their heresy. Mormonism, for example, clearly, relentlessly, and unrepentantly teaches that men may become gods. Latter-day Saints often tell me the Bible validates this teaching when it says, ". . .there be gods many and lords many. . ." (1 Cor. 8:5). They are right, the Bible does say that, but it does not mean that men can become gods. To understand what it really means, you have first to look at its local context, then at its larger context. The local context of a passage of scripture includes the verses immediately before and after it. In this case, we would need to look not only at verse five of First Corinthians, but verses four through six. When we do so we discover the passage is really teaching exactly the opposite of what Latter-day Saints suggest:

> As concerning therefore the eating of those things that are offered in sacrifice unto idols, we know that an idol is nothing in the world, and that there is none other God but one.

> For though there be that are called gods, whether in heaven or in earth, (as there be gods many, and lords many,)

> But to us there is but one God, the Father, of whom are all things, and we in him. . . and one Lord Jesus Christ, by whom are all things, and we by him. (1 Cor. 8:4-6)

Proper context means that the exact meaning of a word is determined by the words immediately surrounding it within in its verse. Beyond that, however, its meaning is determined by its larger context. And beyond that, chapters derive their meaning to some degree from the overall direction of the book within which they are found. In fact, individual books are contextualized within Testaments: you cannot understand the writing of John or Paul if you try to squeeze their theology into the context of the Old Testament without taking into consideration the overall revelation of the New Testament.

When, for example, the Apostle Paul writes that fornicators and adulterers shall not inherit the kingdom of heaven (1 Cor 6:9), we know from the context of the New Testament that he is not saying that anyone who has committed adultery in the past (technically an adulterer) will go to hell. The context of the passage leads us to conclude that he is talking about people who continue in adultery and fornication. Their continuing sin gives evidence to the fact that they are not part of the kingdom of God. To conclude that anyone who commits adultery can never enter the kingdom of heaven ignores the context of the Bible as a whole, that God loves sinners and has provided a way for them to escape the just punishment of their sin.

Without context we cannot hope to understand Benny Hinn nor anyone else. Heresy hunters are willing to grab one or two sentences or paragraphs out of a sermon, tape, TV show, or off-the-record interview and attempt to hang the person making the comments. Such activity is beneath the level of serious apologists.

A rush-to-judgment mentality is common among heresy hunters. They do not view potential doctrinal problems within a man's ministry as an opportunity for dialogue and healing. They do not approach him patiently with the hope of understanding where he is coming from. They really do not want to understand him.

Is Hinn a heretic? Not in the judgment of some theologians. In attempting to make the case that Benny Hinn is heretical about the Trinity, the heresy hunters need to remember that in the opinion of CRI reviewer Robert Bowman, *Good Morning Holy Spirit* stops short of heresy. They need to remember that J. Rodman Williams found *Good Morning Holy Spirit* "very profitable." I suggest that until such time as Hinn is fairly and fully examined, it is intemperate at least, and arrogant at worst, to call him a heretic.

An Opportunity for Repentance

I certainly agree that Benny Hinn would have saved himself and the rest of us a lot of heartburn if he had never made the "nine of them" statement. But the heresy hunters fail to see that Benny Hinn also wishes he had never said it. He said to *Christianity Today*:

> That (the "nine of them" remark) was a very dumb statement. I had read somewhere that God the Father had His own personal spirit, soul, and body. I told my church the very next week that the statement was wrong.[8]

Heresy hunters seem to labor under the idea that only fully educated, perfectly sound theologians are used by God for the work of the ministry. Nothing could be further from the truth. I appreciate scholarship, and I thank God for seminaries, but for every example of how theological education has produced good fruit, it is possible to demonstrate the reverse. How many sincere Christians wind up in seminary only to have their genuine sensitivity to God educated out of them? They may come out of seminary doctrinally sound but spiritually dead. I long for a Church in which all ministers are at once scholarly exact, spiritually alive, emotionally mature, and socially sensitive. In the meantime I'll love and respect men of God who fall short in some of these areas.

Within a week Hinn admitted he was wrong: It was a "dumb" thing to say; it was an ill-conceived remark; he wished he hadn't said it. Part of his mistake was naiveté. He doubtless had no idea people were "monitoring" his sermon—and taping it, ready to distribute it if it contained erroneous statements. Remember, *Christianity Today* said before the publication of *Good Morning Holy Spirit* that "few outside of Charismatic circles had heard of pastor and author Benny Hinn."

We have all heard pastors make theological errors from the pulpit. Some of them stemmed from ignorance. In some cases the pastors need correction. When such correction is given, however, it should be done with fear and trembling. Experience tells us, "All ministry comes to and through broken-hearted people." Church is the place where mistakes can be made. The Lord provides for correction, not simply condemnation.

How Much Is Too Much?

The bottom-line question is "Can a man of God make wrong statements and remain a man of God?" In a perfect Church—one without spot or wrinkle (Eph. 5:27)—preachers would not say wrong or outlandish things. But this isn't such a world, and that isn't the present character of the Church. Preachers sin and fall short of the glory of God. So the question becomes "At what point does the sin or error become great enough to disqualify him from ministry?" Does the "nine of them" quote, in itself, disqualify Hinn from ministry? Especially in light of the fact that he retracted it? The answer is "No, it does not."

In fact, the heresy hunters agree with me. None of them would think to hang Hinn for that single, retracted statement. That brings me to my point: I believe Hinn's style predisposes him to be viewed with repugnance by some members of the Church. The heresy hunters who seek to eject him from ministry seize upon mistakes he would otherwise be forgiven of if his style were different. As Hinn himself puts it, "The problem with becoming well-known is that everything you say and do is subject to scrutiny. Things are taken out of context (and) misunderstood."[9]

It is the predisposition of the heresy hunters to try to find things wrong with those they deem unworthy for ministry. Ever vigilant when their victims do commit a real sin such as the "nine of them" statement, they fasten on it and beat him to death with it. In the "nine of them" case, we can document that the feeding frenzy is a reality. The minute Hinn made the statement, he was jumped on with zeal. *Christianity Today* reports:

> Free-lance journalist William Alnor, who works closely with the California-based Christian Research Institute, had the sermon transcribed and mailed to some twenty-five ministries and media outlets.[10]

The Feeding Frenzy in Action

What *Christianity Today* didn't report however, was that the mailing took place within two days! Alnor mailed a news release on the Monday following the Saturday "nine of them" statement. In the meantime, he had shown the video to "several" theology teachers at Philadelphia College of the Bible (the Bible College founded by C. I. Scofield). This release and the statements of the PCB theologians were immediately circulated to more than two dozen cult-watch groups. I see several things wrong with this.

First, it was hasty. As Hinn told *Christianity Today*: "That was a very dumb statement. I told my church the very next week that the statement was wrong."[11]

In two days Alnor had grabbed the video tape, screened it before a few teachers, and then mailed their reactions to twenty-five ministries. That does not sound like someone who is sincerely interested in correcting Hinn's error; it sounds like someone determined to stop him, a clearly

different act. It is obvious that Alnor's action was a jour-
nalistic tactic, not a fellowship tactic. His photocopied
"news release" is just that—a press release. The news media
orientation of modern apologetics concerns me deeply. It
is an odious replacement for biblical correction.

Alnor's news release is also subjective. It is entitled,
"Leading Charismatic Denies the Historic Doctrine of the
Trinity on National Television." His lead says,

> Benny Hinn—one of America's best-known Charismatic
> leaders—redefined the nature of God and man on his
> Saturday (Oct. 13, 1990) telecast broadcast nation-
> wide on the Trinity Broadcasting Network.[12]

Alnor, while acting as a journalist, cannot resist insert-
ing his own opinion of Hinn's ministry into the news
release. He says:

> Pastor Hinn's view of the invisible side of man is
> unorthodox. . . Hinn was last in the news when an
> elderly lady died after a person "slain in the spirit" by
> Benny Hinn (sic) fell on her, breaking her hip. Her
> family filed a wrongful death suit against the church.[13]

The news release triggered a wide circulation of the
Hinn statements in record time; certainly it was in the
hands of many ministries by the time Hinn corrected
himself publicly before his 7,000 member church the
following week. His correction, however, was not soon
reported by the heresy hunters.

To its credit, *Christianity Today* eventually reported
Hinn's retraction of the "nine of them" remark and other
questionable statements. That was in October 1991. However, by October 1992, *Christianity Today* reported that
Hinn's detractors had concluded that his renunciations
were insincere and had compiled a completely new list of
other problems with him.

String 'Em Together and then String 'Em Up

The feeding frenzy on Hinn escalated into an ava-
lanche of minutia. The theory seems to be "If you don't
have anything truly heretical to report, then string to-

gether a lot of quasi-heretical statements to make their total weight add up to heresy." This is not legitimate. A hundred intemperate statements simply prove the minister is intemperate, not that he is a heretic. I would be willing to stipulate that Benny Hinn is somewhat intemperate. I just can't stipulate he is a heretic; in my opinion, insufficient evidence has been presented to convict him of that.

The 1992 *Christianity Today* article was entitled "Same Old Benny Hinn, Critics Say." No new, substantial doctrinal charges were made against Hinn in the article. His detractors, CRI and PFO, instead accused him of other misdemeanors. For example, they said he intemperately reacted to those who attacked him. Another charge was leveled by Kurt Goedelman of PFO, "You get the idea that (Hinn thinks that) the Holy spirit floods through Benny every day." They also asserted that he had used exaggerated illustrations in his sermons. J. Rodman Williams agreed that Hinn is prone to "extremism" and his exegesis is "frequently unsound" but steadfastly maintained and that he "is a man God is using today."[14]

In my estimation, such claims should fall short of anyone's definition of heresy. Hinn may well be immature and sinful. If so he shares those qualities with me, you, and his detractors. The original charges against Hinn were that he taught heresy. Apparently unable to prove those charges, the heresy hunters determined to prove he is not mature enough to be a preacher. That is a different argument.

It also is a dangerous argument. Who is going to judge preachers on their maturity? Do we have a priesthood screening organization? Are we required to be licensed to preach? If so, who should qualify us—the government, the World Council of Churches, CRI? We need to be very careful when we suggest that someone from the outside can come into a church and disqualify the preacher. Given that kind of meddling, Evangelicals would excommunicate mainline preachers, Pentecostals would oust Fun-

damentalists, seminarians would disqualify those without
formal education, and the refined would disqualify the
common. No, it is one thing to examine a man's doctrine
and morality. It is quite another to attempt to address his
maturity and style.

Such qualities are extremely difficult to assess. Who
among us would have voted to sustain King David as
leader of Israel? He was a murderer and an adulterer.
How many of us would have chosen Noah? The last picture of him in the Bible shows him naked and drunk.
What about Abraham, the Father of Faith? He continually
lied that Sarah was his sister, not his wife, so that Pharaoh
would not kill him. Jonah was a coward; Jeremiah "refused" to preach; Elijah was afraid of Jezebel; Solomon
had a thousand wives and concubines. Or what about the
Apostles? Were they mature when they began their ministries? Who would have chosen Peter? He raised his sword
against the soldiers who arrested Jesus, tried to dissuade
Jesus from the cross (Jesus called him "Satan" when he
did that), and denied Him three times. James and John
sent their mother in an attempt to manipulate Jesus into
guaranteeing them the head positions at the table of God.
Who among us would have been thrilled with the way
John the Baptist ran his ministry?

For that matter, would we have approved of the direction of the ministry of Jesus? He was despised and rejected by his religious critics. Remember, at one point, all
of his followers walked out of his meeting—save only the
twelve disciples. Finally he said to the local religious community:

> But where unto shall I liken this generation? It is like
> unto children sitting in the markets, and calling unto
> their fellows,
>
> And saying, We have piped unto you, and ye have not
> danced; we have mourned unto you, and ye have not
> lamented.
>
> For John came neither eating nor drinking, and they
> say, He hath a devil.

The Son of man came eating and drinking, and they
say, Behold a man gluttonous, and a winebibber, a
friend of publicans and sinners. (Matt. 11:16–19)

I wonder why those who oppose Hinn so violently are
unimpressed by the fact that thousands of Christians (including hundreds of pastors and teachers and not a few
theologians) stand behind him? I know of dozens of educated, saved, humble ministers who enjoy Hinn's preaching and say they are edified by his anointing. Many of
these men say they recognize a genuine humility in Benny
Hinn. Hinn frequently, and in my opinion sincerely, says
of himself, "I am nothing. It is only Jesus who can heal
you or help you."

True, many of us cringe when he makes "dumb" statements. Remember he said that before the Fall, Adam
could fly! Now, I do not happen to think Adam could fly
before the Fall, but, on sober reflection, I'm not absolutely sure he couldn't! Scripture seems to be silent on
that issue. I can extrapolate that since men are not observed to be able fly in this fallen world, it was impossible
that any could have in an unfallen one. But then I think
of Philip the evangelist and his quick trip to Azotus after
baptizing the Ethiopian eunuch, and I'm not so sure. So
I say, "Who cares?" I might care if it were a major doctrinal part of Hinn's teaching, but it isn't. It is simply a
statement made in passing in the heat of sermonizing. I
prefer to let it go.

Remember the Agenda

Why can't heresy hunters let such statements go?
Because they have an agenda. Once they are convinced
that Hinn or anyone else needs to be taken out of ministry, they nose through his statements like bloodhounds.
They are not studying doctrinal dissertations and thinking
through thorny postulates from theologians; they have
decided to be the watchdogs of the Church, deciding
whom you and I should listen to on television and where
we should attend church.

I have no objections when apologists want to write about the Trinity or the faith movement. I have no problem when they "name names,"—if it is in the context of simply pointing to examples of where suspect doctrines are being taught. But when ministers set themselves to "take out" other ministers, alarm bells should go off in the Church.

Prejudice is not the same as reason and logic. Prejudice is not justice. Prejudice simply identifies those who are "different" and labels them as unworthy. If Benny Hinn is not a genuine heretic but is instead simply a peculiar preacher, those who want to disfellowship him do so at the peril of depriving the Church of one of its most effective evangelists.

CHAPTER 5

Sins of Pride

Some heresy hunters are motivated by a basic theological difference between themselves and those they attack. One of the most strident examples of heresy hunting comes from those who believe the manifestation of certain spiritual gifts has ceased. Those who take that position do not think Benny Hinn's "slaying in the Spirit," Bob Larson's "exorcisms," Oral Robert's miraculous "faith-healings," or Pat Robertson's "words of knowledge" are genuine manifestations of the Holy Spirit. They are not genuine, because in the minds of some of their critics, they are not possible.

The debate between "Fundamentalists" and "Pentecostals" has caused misunderstanding throughout most of this century. The issue is cloudy because Pentecostals think of themselves as very "fundamental" in theology: They believe in the inerrancy of scripture, the new birth, and all the other fundamentals of the faith. However, they do not always realize that true Fundamentalists view the Pentecostal experience with varying degrees of skepticism.

As a matter of fact, a formal break occurred in the Evangelical community in 1928 when Pentecostals were barred from the World's Christian Fundamentalist Association. The resolution that disfellowshipped them stated:

> Whereas the present wave of Modern Pentecostalism,
> often referred to as the "tongues movement," and the

present wave of fanatical and unscriptural healing which is sweeping over the country today, has become a menace in many churches and a real injury to sane testimony of Fundamental Christians, be it resolved that this convention go on record as unreservedly opposed to Modern Pentecostalism.[1]

As we shall see, the division has not entirely healed. In spite of attempts to simply put the differences behind us, the fact is, they do not seem to go away.

Observation reveals two obvious points: First, most of those under fire from modern heresy hunters are Charismatics; and second, the heresy charges against them usually involve some aspect of Pentecostal/Charismatic thinking.

Perhaps it would be more correct to say that one of the basic differences in the dispute stems from a conflict over the roles of rationalism and emotionalism in Christian experience. The heresy hunters tend to believe that much of what Charismatics call "spiritual" is nothing more than emotionalism.

It is not that the heresy hunters think God is without emotion, but they see Him as primarily rational. They are right when they say that Charismatics stress the relational—or emotional—connection Christians make to God as a result of conversion. Charismatics do indeed see salvation as an "experience" as well as a rational decision.

The emotional/rational debate has always been at the heart of controversy during times of spiritual outpouring. Those who puzzle over the motives of heresy hunters will return, again and again, to this dilemma.

As I said, many heresy hunters deny they are motivated in the ways I have described. They often profess no bias against Pentecostalism. To help explain why I distrust these denials, I need to present a brief overview of the history of the Pentecostal/Charismatic Movements.

The Pentecostal Movement began at the turn of the twentieth century when individuals within the so-called "Holiness Movement" began to experience manifestations

of the Holy Spirit such as speaking in tongues, prophecy,
and physical healings. As I mentioned in chapter 1, many
of these same phenomena accompanied the Great Awakening. They also occurred in the Second Great Awakening (c. 1787-1825). Nevertheless, Pentecostal expression
in our modern era can be dated to 1 January 1901, when
certain students of Charles F. Parham's Bible school in
Topeka, Kansas, began speaking in tongues.

At first, Pentecostals were simply ignored as fanatics,
but soon their opponents developed a formal anti-Pentecostal theology. The argument against Pentecostalism, developed mainly within the Fundamentalist movement, was
that miraculous gifts were not given to the Church for all
time but were divine manifestations for unique periods of
time—notably the First Century A.D. The argument was
(and is) that the gifts were given by God to the Apostles
only to establish the Church, and subsequently they were
withdrawn. Once the Bible canon was established, the
argument goes, the gifts were unnecessary. The proof text
for this position is found in the book of First Corinthians,
chapter thirteen:

> Charity never faileth: but whether there be prophe-
> cies, they shall fail; whether there be tongues, they
> shall cease; whether there be knowledge, it shall van
> ish away.
>
> For we know in part, and we prophesy in part.
>
> But when that which is perfect is come, then that
> which is in part shall be done away (1 Cor. 13:8-10).

The Fundamentalists fastened on the phrase, "when
that which is perfect is come," and said that it referred to
the completion of the biblical canon. They concluded
that, since the "perfect had come," tongues and prophecy
were "done away" with. (For inexplicable reasons, Fundamentalists did not think "knowledge" was done away with.)
Pentecostals, of course, rejected these interpretations. They
said "the perfect" could only refer to the eventual return
of Christ—not the Bible.

The second Fundamentalist argument is an argument

from experience: since gifts of the Spirit were seldom observed in the American churches prior to the twentieth century, the anti-Pentecostal argument went, those gifts were obviously removed by God. This is an ironic argument: One of the primary charges made against the Pentecostals was that their theology resulted from their experience. Now those who opposed the Pentecostals did so on the basis of their own experience (or rather, lack of experience).

The Fundamentalist/Pentecostal debate kept the two movements separated and marked Pentecostalism as a pariah for decades. However, events in the 1950s introduced the modern Charismatic Movement to the Body of Christ when Pentecostal manifestations such as speaking in tongues began to break out within mainline churches like the Episcopal Church pastored by Dennis Bennett in Van Nuys, California. Soon the manifestations began occurring in Presbyterian, Lutheran, and Catholic churches as well as in virtually every other denomination.

The initial reaction to the Charismatic outbreak was to be expected—fear and resentment. Soon, however, it became apparent that "Charismania" was here to stay. In 1977, 50,000 Charismatics from dozens of denominations met in conference in Kansas City, Missouri. At the same time, Charismatics took important positions in Christian media: Pat Robertson founded the Christian Broadcasting Network, and, at the same time, Charismatic Christian magazines like *Charisma* became important members of the Christian press. As the movement spread, it became obvious to much of the rest of the Church that God was in it. Charismatics became not only welcome but respected members of the Evangelical community; men like Jack Hayford, pastor of a large Pentecostal Church in Van Nuys, California, were invited to speak at the mid-July 1989 Second Lausanne Conference on World Evangelism in Manila, where Charismatics participated with non-Charismatics on equal footing.[2] With the general acceptance of the Charismatic Movement by the larger Body of

Christ, the more moderate wing of Fundamentalism was forced to tone down its most strenuous objections and adopt a somewhat modified position. It continued to be uneasy with Charismania but refrained from suggesting it was from the devil.

Anti-Charismatic Prejudice

But not everyone gives up so easily. Some Fundamentalists defend the position that the Pentecostal/Charismatic Movement is foundationally heretical. They go so far as to suggest that, though Charismatics may "love the Lord," they are deeply deceived by the devil.

John MacArthur, pastor of the thriving Grace Community Church in Sun Valley, California, is convinced that Charismatic theology is flawed to its core. MacArthur, in many ways, typifies the anti-Charismatic bias of much of the Evangelical community. That bias drives much of the heresy hunting activities.

MacArthur is one of the most highly esteemed Fundamentalists in the country. He is the author of numerous books and has a national radio program, "Grace to You." In 1978 MacArthur first wrote about the Charismatic movement. He authored *The Charismatics: A Doctrinal Perspective*, which was decidedly anti-Charismatic in tone. At that time I was just entering pastoral ministry. I was interested in MacArthur's position not only because I was a Charismatic, but because I recognized him to be a respected pastor-teacher. In fact, I used his teaching tapes to train my own church leadership.

I was, however, disappointed in *The Charismatics*. My overriding reaction to it was, "I wish John knew personally the Charismatics I know!" His book described, in my opinion, a caricature of the Charismatic movement. I thought he used the worst examples of Charismatic foolishness he could find. For example, he mentions a letter he got from a woman who claimed she had taught her dog "to praise the Lord in an unknown bark." I wondered how he would have responded to a similar caricature of the worst of Fundamentalism.

However, *The Charismatics* found a large audience.
Apparently many Christians related to the picture of the
off-the-wall, "super-spiritual" individual who MacArthur
described as the average Charismatic. *The Charismatics*
attempted to defend the classic Fundamentalist position
that the gifts had ceased. Nevertheless, the Charismatic/
Pentecostal movement continued to prosper. In 1991,
MacArthur revised the book under the title *Charismatic
Chaos*. As suggested by the title, the revision was even
more anti-Charismatic than the original. He repeats the
"unknown bark" story and says that the decade that passed
between the two editions of the book only confirms that
the praising dog is typical of Charismatics' experience.

MacArthur's book repeats the Fundamentalist position: He argues that miracles, including miraculous
healings, do not occur within the Charismatic Movement
today. (He believes miracles have only occurred in three
very specific eras during human history and that all manifestations of the miraculous ceased after the Apostolic
Age.) He suggests the Charismatic claim that God speaks
prophetically through people today means that Charismatics equate those prophecies with scripture, and that
Charismatics define truth by their experience, not by the
Word of God. He suggests that those who speak in tongues
do so either demonically, or in a psychologically induced
state similar to hypnosis, or simply obediently as a learned
behavior.

It is not my purpose, nor is it possible within the
scope of this book, to defend the Charismatic Movement
against the claims of MacArthur or others. It is enough to
understand that as much as MacArthur may dissent, the
Church at large considers the phenomena of Pentecost to
be valid. Please understand that I respect MacArthur's
right to disagree with Pentecostal theology. He not only
has every right to do that, but as an honorable pastor, he
has the responsibility to point out what he believes is
error. No, I am not objecting to his Fundamentalist argu-

ments. I am objecting again to the way in which he makes
them.

MacArthur's Methods

Charismatic Chaos cites the most bizarre examples of
foolish behavior to illustrate what MacArthur thinks is
Charismatic theology. This is unfair. If I were to pick out
every red-necked, uneducated, foolish Fundamentalist
preacher I could find and hold him up as an example of
Fundamentalism, I would be guilty not only of the worst
possible journalism but also of wreaking spiritual havoc.
If I were to characterize Fundamentalism as a bunch of
spiritual exclusivists who thrived on conspiracy theories
and turned their wives into doormats and alienated their
children, I would be guilty of rumor-mongering and spiritual division. That is what MacArthur has done by deliberately choosing the most extreme examples of foolishness, examples which do not typify the experience of the
normal, Bible-believing Charismatic.

When MacArthur uses such extreme tactics to make
his point, he is not simply on a personal vendetta. On the
contrary, his views represent a large segment of the Evangelical community.

Experience or Scripture?

MacArthur believes Charismatics—by and large—test
all spiritual events, not by the Bible, but by their own
experience. In fact, this is MacArthur's most foundational
definition of what it means to be a Charismatic. For example, MacArthur recounts a story from a very obscure
newsletter about a man who claims to have been trans-
ported to heaven for five-and a-half days. The man report-
edly said there were horses in heaven, "all praising God."
(MacArthur appears to be fascinated with "praising animal" stories told by Charismatics.) MacArthur then says:

> Charismatics have no way to judge or stop testimo-
> nies like that because in their system experience vali-
> dates itself. Instead of checking such experiences

against the Bible for validity, typically Charismatics
try to get the Bible to fit the experience or, failing
that, they just ignore the Bible.[3]

I do not deny that such heaven-and-back stories are
heard within the Charismatic Movement. In addition, many
similar stories, prophecies, and other events are reported.
But to suggest that Pentecostal theology "has no way to
judge" such things must mean MacArthur is either ignorant of what Charismatics really believe, or that he is
being less than fair in his reporting. Responsible Charismatic leaders say they exercise great care in these matters.
And they believe the Bible does, indeed, tell them how to
deal with prophecy. I quote only one scripture which is
part of the theological basis for their discernment:

> When you come together, everyone has a hymn, or a
> word of instruction, a revelation, a tongue or an in-
> terpretation. All of these must be done for the strength-
> ening of the church. If anyone speaks in a tongue,
> two—or at the most three—should speak, one at a
> time, and someone must interpret. If there is no in-
> terpreter, the speaker should keep quiet in the church
> and speak to himself and God. Two or three prophets
> should speak, and the others should weigh carefully
> (*judge*—KJV) what is said. (1 Cor. 14:26-29 NIV)

Many Charismatic pastors use this passage to lead
their congregations in the exercising of spiritual gifts. For
MacArthur to suggest that Pentecostal leadership has not
thought about these matters is ludicrous. For him to make
such a basic mistake about the Charismatic movement
calls into question his ability to comment objectively on
this subject.

Do Charismatics Think They Are Superior to Other Christians?

MacArthur's concept of how Charismatics view themselves and other Christians is warped. But it seems to be
typical of too many Fundamentalists. He displays his prejudice when he accuses Charismatics, in general, of feeling
they are spiritually superior to other Christians, he writes:

Charismatics generally believe that after someone
becomes a Christian, he or she must seek diligently
for the baptism of the Spirit. Those who get this
baptism also experience various phenomena, such as
speaking in tongues, feelings of euphoria, visions, and
emotional outbursts of various kinds. Those who have
not experienced the baptism and its accompanying
phenomena are not considered Spirit-filled; that is
they are immature, carnal, disobedient, or otherwise
incomplete Christians.[4]

Such generalized stereotyping of Charismatic opinion
is not only inaccurate, but it also widens the gulf between
Charismatics and Fundamentalists. This view of Charismatics may cause them, especially Charismatic leaders, to
adopt a "siege mentality." This can feed and escalate the
original misunderstanding about them on the part of the
heresy hunters.

Although some Charismatics may believe that all non-
Charismatics are "immature, carnal, disobedient, or otherwise incomplete," it is not the typical viewpoint. Pentecostal theology certainly views the Baptism of the Holy
Spirit as a tremendously valuable encounter which opens
a doorway to important spiritual experience. Charismatics
defend that experience and hope to share it with others.
For MacArthur to suggest, however, that Charismatics
generally disdain those who do not receive the experience
is—again—either ignorance or misrepresentation. Let me
make a comparison. Lutherans believe the center of normal worship experience should be the celebration of Holy
Communion—and they are not afraid to say so. They
might even think that less liturgical Christians are missing
something—and are, in that sense, "incomplete." However, that does not mean they think that other Christians
are immature, carnal, or disobedient. Viewing your theology as vital, healthy, and even "right" is not the same as
viewing the theology of others as insipid, unhealthy and
wrong. MacArthur's rhetoric is not helpful.

MacArthur is convinced Charismatics hold scripture
in low esteem. This misconception may cause him and

others to make the mistake of thinking their own scholarship is generally superior to that of Charismatics. MacArthur again quotes an out-of-context paragraph—this time from another obscure source—to prove that Charismatics have a low view of scripture. He quotes the following from a book entitled *Miraculous Healing*:

> It may be anticipated, as the present apostasy increases, that Christ will manifest His deity and lordship in increasing measure through miracle-signs, including healings. We are not to say, therefore, that the word is sufficient.

MacArthur reacts with indignation to this passage. He responds:

> Not to say that Scripture is sufficient? God Himself says His Word is sufficient! (Ps. 19:7-14; 2 Tim. 3:15-17). Who is Henry Frost to claim that it is not?[5]

That is an excellent question. I, for one, had no idea who Henry Frost was/is. I had never heard of him. I checked Zondervan's *Dictionary of Pentecostal and Charismatic Movements* and discovered he is not listed there although hundreds of other Charismatic leaders are. The book MacArthur is quoting was published in 1937! Certainly, regardless of who Frost was, his book, written twenty years before the first stirring of the Charismatic movement, is not a good source to use as a discussion of Charismatic theology. Why does MacArthur choose such an obscure source to typify what Charismatics believe about scripture? Worse, Frost's passage is quoted without context. I'll have to take MacArthur's word that the "word" that Frost is referring to is the Bible.

Having given us this out-of-context, obscure snippet, MacArthur reacts to it as though it had great meaning. Then he uses it to validate his own conviction that: "Although most Charismatics would not state their position as clearly as Frost, the truth is, at the core of their belief system is a denial of Scripture's sufficiency."[6]

Again and again MacArthur claims what all thinking Charismatics firmly deny—that Pentecostals hold scripture in low esteem. MacArthur fails to prove his point, but he remains adamant in his belief: "Charismatics have abandoned the uniqueness of Scripture as the only Word of God, and the result is a spiritual free for all."[7]

MacArthur is not simply critical of excesses in the Charismatic movement. He clearly believes it is not of God at all. He calls Charismatic theology "pseudo-Christian mysticism."[8] He says "many in the charismatic movement are perilously close to Neo-Baalism."[9] He further says: "I am convinced that the fundamental teachings of the charismatic movement. . . encourage bogus claims, false prophets, and other forms of spiritual humbug."[10]

For MacArthur, the Charismatic experience is all foolishness. He says the gift of tongues being spoken today by Charismatics is "not biblical": "Those who speak in tongues today are not practicing the gift described in Scripture."[11]

He maintains that the gift of tongues is either "Satanic, neurotic, or simply learned behavior."[12] His opinion of Charismatics is epitomized by his use of numerous weird examples. It all comes back to the "unknown bark" and the "praising horses." One such example so strains my ability to believe that I think it is worth including. I think it illustrates that MacArthur is not interested in understanding Charismatics but in ridiculing the Movement:

> I talked with one charismatic who said, "Oh, yes, it's vital to be slain in the Spirit. In fact, you should never go for more than two or three weeks without being slain in the Spirit." A former charismatic told me there are no limits to it. It often becomes a contest to see who can get "slain" the most often.[13]

But It's Not Just the Methods

It is not just MacArthur's methodology, however, that concerns me. His methodology raises questions about his motivation. He challenges an entire movement made up of dozens of respected denominations. His challenge is different from the other heresy hunters in that he does

not limit his criticism to those he views as individual
misfits within the movement. He challenges the movement itself. In rejecting such a broad segment of the
Church, he—knowingly or unknowingly—sets himself above
the council of the larger Church. Is he, I wonder, both-
ered by the fact that other evangelicals, such as Billy
Graham and Charles Colson, have not discovered that the
Charismatic movement is typified by bogus claims and
spiritual humbug?

I am very reluctant to speak to his motivation; I see
only his actions, not his heart. As a matter of fact, it is very
difficult for me to believe that MacArthur is, at heart,
proud and arrogant. Nevertheless, we must recognize that
his work escalates the anti-Charismatic prejudice into new
realms. Let's view this from the opposite perspective: if I
were to suggest that Fundamentalism is demonic in origin
or that its foundation is spiritually dangerous, I would be
flying in the face of the entire Evangelical Church. Such
a declaration would suggest that I felt my judgment was
better than that of the best minds and most pious Christians of our day. If I set out—as John MacArthur seem-
ingly has done—to demonstrate that a segment of the
Church is fatally flawed at its core, I should be prepared
to demonstrate that.

MacArthur is well within the borders of propriety
when he states his opinion that miracles ceased after the
first century A.D. It is a theory he believes. He should, of
course, state his reasons for his belief in that position. But
remember, it is only his belief. God may disagree with
him. His defense of Fundamentalism and his criticism of
Pentecostalism is healthy when it speaks to the theology.
It is unhealthy when it ridicules Charismatic practice.

In the end, we must wonder what his imbalanced
attack on the Charismatic communion has accomplished.
Misrepresentation and exaggeration do, indeed, inflame
the heresy hunters; however, such tactics do not add to
the work of evangelism set before the Church. In fact,
such tactics serve only to weaken and divide the Church.

CHAPTER 6

Sins of Jealousy

I am especially sensitive about heresy hunting because I saw firsthand the damage done to a colleague by self-appointed critics who attacked him because of a book he and I co-authored. As time went on, they shifted the focus from the book to my friend's character. Eventually they even attacked the character of the man he worked for!

No amount of reason could convince the attackers that they were making a mistake. Months turned into years, and the attacks only stopped after I published a full account of their unreasonable position.[1] The cost, however, was high, and in defending my friends, I was accused by others of "fighting with the brethren."

This experience doubtless sensitized me to the feelings of ministers who suffer at the hands of heresy hunters.

Although God brought my friends and me through the siege, I shall never forget the bitterness of the attack, nor the confusion it created. Supporters who knew and respected our ministries could not help thinking, "where there is smoke there must be fire."

After nearly three years of wrangling with this tiny band of heresy hunters, their attack culminated in my colleagues' and my being characterized as "irresponsible cult-bashers" in a major book on the cults. The author who penned those words had never met me, had never (I'm certain) read my books, had never spoken to any pastor of a church where I had ministered, but had relied solely upon the words of the heresy hunters. I tried in vain to contact the author, and I appealed in vain to the publisher to review and change the statement about me.

The Temple of Doom

It all began in 1987 when I co-authored a booklet entitled *Mormonism's Temple of Doom* with Bill Schnoebelen. The book grew out of Bill's testimony about his conversion to Christ out of Mormonism and witchcraft. I was interested in Bill's testimony because I had long considered the occult rituals of the Mormon temple ceremony to be a cornerstone of that organization's theological structure, and Bill's experiences confirmed my belief.

I met Bill at a Capstone Conference in Salt Lake City. This was an annual gathering of those involved in ministry to Mormons that was organized by Ed Decker, author of the book *The God Makers* and founder of Saints Alive!, an organization that seeks to evangelize Latter-day Saints.

Ed was growing more vocal in his contention that a root problem of Mormonism was its occult history. He asked Bill to speak to the conference about the Mormon/occult connection.

Bill told a fantastic story of religious addiction. Raised in a Catholic home, he eventually received a master's degree in religion from a Catholic university. However, he had also become involved in witchcraft and had studied the black arts in depth. In the course of his religious quest, he had joined numerous occult organizations and progressed through the higher degrees of Freemasonry. In addition, he had read most of the major literature on the occult. He had even studied Satanism and joined Anton Szandor LaVey's Church of Satan. Eventually, Bill joined the Mormon Church. When he went through the Mormon temple ceremony, he discovered that it was thoroughly occult in nature.

Then in 1984, after years of wading through occult religious experience, Bill was born again by the grace of God. During those few days at the conference, I began thinking that we should publish his testimony, particularly as it related to his experience with the temple ceremony. I felt he was uniquely qualified to comment on the ceremony's occult significance.

I invited Bill to accompany me to Billings, Montana, to be part of a seminar on Mormonism I was doing there. We spent almost sixteen hours in the car as we traveled, as well as the time between meetings. I became convinced that Bill was a sincere, honest man who happened to possess a unique background which made him especially useful in pointing out the occult roots of the Mormon temple ceremony.

We released *Mormonism's Temple of Doom* at the Capstone Conference at Park City, Utah, the following year. The main speaker at that conference was the late Walter Martin, noted apologist and founder of the Christian Research Institute. Walter was affectionately known as "The Bible Answer Man," which was the title of his nationally syndicated radio show. Ed Decker and I took Walter to the airport at the close of the convention. On the way I gave Walter a copy of our book. When I returned to the hotel in Park City later that night, I had a message to call Walter at his home. He told me he had read the book and wanted me to rush two hundred copies to him. He began to make it available through his ministry.

The Attack on Mormonism's Temple of Doom

The main thrust of our book was to demonstrate that the Mormon temple ceremony was occult in origin. We documented our claims by describing the ceremony and explaining the occult significance of it. We talked about the secret temple clothing and the blasphemous statements temple participants were forced to utter. We published detailed pictures of the blood oaths—pictures that showed the practitioner's thumb to his throat as he swore never to reveal the secret handshakes of Mormonism. In the actual ceremony, the participant would place his right thumb under his left ear while swearing, "I (new secret temple name) promise never to reveal the first token of the Aaronic Priesthood. Rather than do so, I would suffer my life to be taken."

The participant was then required to draw his thumb across his throat, signifying the ritualistic slitting of his throat. Similar oaths required the symbolic disemboweling of the temple participant. All of these blood oaths were compared to near exact copies of them found in both Freemasonry and witchcraft. In fact we showed pictures of the handshakes (Masonic and witchcraft "grips") side-by-side with the nearly identical Mormon "tokens."

Admittedly, this was heavy stuff. However, we were convinced that for some people only such plain talk would be understood. In the introduction to *Mormonism's Temple of Doom*, I stated:

> Many gracious people who have read my first two books. . . have told me how much they appreciated my compassionate approach to Latter-day Saints. My motive in writing the books was to attempt to create an atmosphere in which they could hear the gospel of Christ. . .
>
> My motivation has not changed in this current work. I want to expose the roots of Mormonism which, I have increasingly come to see, are occult. I believe that it is impossible to reach Latter-day Saints effectively until they have lost confidence in Mormonism. That, I believe requires confrontation. As G. K. Chesterton said:
>
> There is a notion abroad that to win a man we must agree with him. Actually, the opposite is true. Each generation has had to be converted by the man who contradicted it most. The man who is going in a wrong direction will never be set right by the affable religionist who falls into step beside him and goes the same way. Someone must place himself across the path and insist that the straying man turn around and go in the right direction.

The first hint that at least one ministry to Mormons was not happy with our book came in September when

Jerald and Sandra Tanner published an article in their
newsletter, the "Salt Lake City Messenger." The article
was entitled "Devil's All Over." In it the Tanners, themselves former Mormons who are well respected for their
considerable work in opposing the doctrinal errors of
Mormonism, said, "Some critics of the Mormon Church
have become so obsessed with finding 'Luciferian' influence in the temple ceremony that they have lost sight of
reality."

The Tanners named Ed Decker, Bill Schnoebelen,
and *Mormonism's Temple of Doom* as examples. They said
they thought our activities would only "harden the hearts
of the Mormon people against Christians working among
them." Certainly they were entitled to their opinion, and
they were entitled to state it publicly. However, we were
shocked that they failed to talk to us first before they
made statements about our work that could confuse
people. I was particularly mystified by the Tanners' objec-
tion to our book because they themselves had previously
published a booklet on the same subject that seemed
more harsh than *Mormonism's Temple of Doom*. I immediately wrote to them and reminded them that in their
book, *Mormonism, Magic, and Masonry*, they had reported
that the founder of Mormonism, Joseph Smith, had ritually sacrificed sheep in occult rituals. They described the
incidences in a chapter entitled, "Blood Sacrifices for the
Demons."

I was particularly concerned about the Tanners' attack
on our credibility because they sent their mailing to nearly
every anti-cult ministry of significance. I was even more
concerned because the most prominent ministry heads in
our association had spent an entire afternoon at Capstone
Conference discussing how we should—and should not—
deal with each other when disagreements arose. In my
letter to the Tanners I wrote:

> I cannot help but wonder how it is you can publicly
> rebuke brethren without first at least corresponding

with them. We spent an entire afternoon at the
Capstone Coalition meeting discussing how these
matters should be handled. We determined that brothers should never be held up to public criticism without first doing everything possible to make things
right.

Ed and Bill immediately wrote a letter to the Tanners.
In it they said:

We are in something of a dilemma. We highly regard
you both, and Ed especially appreciates the warm
association he has had through the years with Sandra.
However, the article and an audio tape by Jerald, take
serious exception to our work. In fact, the article is a
direct challenge to our honesty, integrity, scholarship,
and mental state. It implies fraud.

Because of the scope of your audience and the fact
that these charges were published broadly, without
any effort to first discuss the issues with us personally,
we feel that it is wise to attempt some sort of Biblical
reconciliation before having this issue go any further.

None of the three of us realized that while we were
corresponding with the Tanners in hopes of putting our
differences to rest, they were producing, at the very
moment our letters had reached their hands, another, this
time more virulent, broadside against us. Before the ink
was dry on our letters to them, they published a twenty-
four-page booklet called *The Lucifer-God Doctrine*. In this
document they again raised questions about our methodology. The Tanners seemed to be most convinced that
our work, "even if (it causes) several thousand people to
leave the Mormon Church," might turn off thousands of
others.[2]

In their booklet, the subject of the attack quickly shifted
from a discussion of the issues (which is, to this day, still
difficult to define precisely) to personalities. The attack
became an *ad hominem* argument. The very way in which
the booklet was structured underscored the Tanners' belief that Bill was a person who could not be trusted. Why,
I wondered, would Bill be subject to such treatment?

What was the point? As time went on, the issues became less and less important and the person of Bill became more important. Eventually they turned the *ad hominem* argument upon Ed Decker, seriously questioning his integrity. Eventually my own integrity would be questioned. In *The Lucifer-God Doctrine*, the Tanners made these statements notable for their innuendo:

> Mr. Schnoebelen claims to have had a deep involvement in the occult. . . claims that after he went into witchcraft, he changed his name. . . claims to have received a Master's Degree from the Saint Francis Seminary in Milwaukee.[5]

All of these claims were verified by the Tanners, and they admit it in the booklet, but the repeated use of the word *claim* was highly prejudicial. The Tanners also said, "William Schnoebelen's writings show that he is given to finding all kinds of trivial parallels between witchcraft and Mormonism."[4]

The Tanners, of course, knew that Schnoebelen was not alone in the documentation of the parallels, which were not at all trivial. As I have noted, the Tanners themselves authored a book on the subject. The most complete book, however, was written by an active Mormon, a Brigham Young University historian named D. Michael Quinn. Quinn's 300-page book, *Early Mormonism and the Magic World View*, not only documents our claim of the Mormon-witchcraft connection but also provides forty pages of photographs and a sixty-page bibliography. The theme of the book is that Mormonism is founded in witchcraft (which he and other Mormon scholars call "folk magic.") It is impossible for me to understand how a conservative Christian could look at the text of the Mormon temple ceremony and not discern that it is occult to its roots.

The Tanners, in fact, do not deny the occult roots of Mormonism. For that reason, we were astounded that when we made our claims, we suddenly found ourselves under attack from them. Not only did they attack the book, but they also attacked it repeatedly. They told us they wanted us to take it out of print. They would be satisfied with nothing less. When we did not submit to their wishes, they began a vicious attack upon Bill's character.

We tried everything we could to satisfy the Tanners. Bill Schnoebelen and I went to Salt Lake City and met with them personally. What we thought would be a meeting to try to end the confusion was instead a "fishing expedition" designed to uncover more evidence to support their unwavering position that Bill was a habitual liar. We were shocked that almost immediately afterwards they twisted what he had said at the meeting (we have the four hours of audio tapes) and published yet another twenty-four-page article designed to blacken his reputation. Before it was over, *The Lucifer-God Doctrine* would be expanded to nearly one hundred pages, none of which had any more substantial evidence than the first attacks.

Their assaults included increasingly wild charges against Ed and Bill. As I said, the ordeal finally seemed to end after I published a detailed and documented report of their tactics, but unfortunately, it didn't end for Ed Decker. In recent years they have leveled even more charges and criticisms against him that are more outlandish than the first ones.

What Was the Problem Anyway?

Unbelievable as it sounds, after years of haggling with the Tanners, I still do not understand why they wanted the book withdrawn from publication. It was one of the most confusing, laborious exercises in futility I have ever engaged in and cost me hundreds of hours of perplexity and misery. I am very sorry to say that after all the wasted time, the best answer I can come up with is that they simply did not like Ed Decker's ministry to Mormons. I also believe they did not like his style. They thought he was too flamboyant and too "unscholarly." I think they genuinely thought he would somehow hurt the overall ministry to Mormons.

Ed Decker, by 1987, had become the recognized leader of the so-called "anti-Mormon" ministry. That term—anti-Mormon is misleading. All of the serious ministers I know within the anti-cult ministries feel a tremendous love for people who are in the cults. They see them as victims. All of us, including Ed Decker and the Tanners, want nothing more than to see Latter-day Saints born again out of Mormonism.

Ed Decker is, indeed, a lightning-rod. His movie, *The God Makers*, was extremely successful in exposing the errors of Mormonism and caused quite a furor in the Mormon community. His second movie, *God Makers II*, is even more controversial—this kind of ministry, by the way, is no picnic. People who disagree with Mormonism have been killed by super-zealots. Blood atonement (the doctrine of ritualistically spilling the blood of sinners) was practiced by Brigham Young and is still practiced in Mormon fundamentalist groups to this day. Many of us have received death threats for our work in this field. The Tanners, in a sense, are probably in the most dangerous position because they are not only well-known "anti-Mormons," but they also live and work in Salt Lake City. But I would not be honest if I did not say that I think part of the Tanners' reaction to *Mormonism's Temple of Doom*, to Bill Schnoebelen, and to Ed Decker was simple jealousy. Again, I know it is difficult to judge motives. So I will admit that I may be wrong. However, nothing else makes sense. The charges against the book did not make sense. The vicious attack on the characters of Bill and Ed did not make sense.

Vindication

History eventually proved us right in a remarkable way. After *Mormonism's Temple of Doom* had been in print a couple of years, the Mormon Church quietly introduced a drastically edited temple ceremony. Many of the changes were alterations to the most disturbing temple practices that we had addressed in our book. For example, the Church removed the blood oaths (along with the arrogant practice of ridiculing Protestant pastors) from the temple ceremony.

A dramatic event occurred in October of 1991 to demonstrate that we had not been overzealous in our unmasking of the occult roots of Mormonism. The *Salt Lake Tribune* carried a front page article that stated that a high-placed Mormon official had admitted that many Mormons were connecting the temple ceremony to Satanism. Bishop Glenn L. Pace, Second Counselor in the Presiding Bishopric of the Mormon Church, said he had personally interviewed more than sixty victims of satanic ritual abuse. The victims were all Mormons who reported witnessing or participating in hideous satanic rituals that were imitations of portions of the temple ceremonies. The rituals, Pace said, were performed by "Mormon leaders, temple workers, and members of the famed Mormon Tabernacle Choir."[5]

Response to our book has been gratifying; several ministries now order it regularly for their work. Many Christian bookstores carry it on their shelves. We have received calls and letters from ministries who are winning Latter-day Saints out of Mormonism and to Christ with the help of our book—and from Mormons who were able to leave the cult as a result of reading the book. (I hasten to add that other forces besides our book doubtless persuaded the Church to drop the blood oaths, but it is undeniable that our book was a major factor in the church's decision.)

The Tanners were wrong to attack our efforts. However, their efforts to discredit us and stifle the book were never based on any evidence of error in our research, but it was based on their distaste for us and for our methods.

If we had acceded to their goal by withdrawing the book, impact on Mormonism would never have occurred, and many souls would still be in bondage. We had the resources and the will to prevail where other ministries wouldn't or couldn't. God only knows how many messages of hope have been destroyed by these kinds of personal attacks.

Heresy hunters can do great damage to the Body of Christ. In this case, they hindered the work of several valuable ministries. They confused the real issue and took people away from the real work of winning souls to answer ridiculous and frivolous accusations. Stirring up contention and creating division in the body of Christ is the poisonous fruit of heresy hunting.

CHAPTER 7

Ethnic Cleansing

The head of the Christian Research Institute, Hank Hanegraaff, says he knows who the "worst of all" false teachers is. Referring to this great heretic, Hanegraaff told his nation-wide radio audience:

> This guy does not belong as a teacher in the Church. He is a false teacher, the worst of all false teachers, and we've been dealing with the cults for thirty years. . . He is fooling millions of people and doing so at quite a profitable rate.[1]

The false teacher who Hanegraaff apparently feels is a worse heretic than Arius, Joseph Smith, or Sun Myung Moon is none other than television evangelist Kenneth Copeland.

Hanegraaff identifies Copeland as one of the "Faith Teachers." The Faith Teachers, Hanegraaff says, are epitomized by Copeland and his mentor Kenneth Hagin. They include others like Benny Hinn, Fred Price, Charles Capps, Jerry Savelle, John Avanzini, Robert Tilton, and Marilyn Hickey.[2] According to Hanegraaff these ministers "mock traditional Christianity" and "completely trash the atonement of Jesus Christ upon the cross."[3]

CRI says each of these people (named above) can: "rightly be considered a cult leader. . . their teachings (can be) regarded as cultic, (and). . . their ardent followers (can be) categorized as cultists."[4]

The *Christian Research Journal* (Winter 1993) contained an article by Hank Hanegraaff entitled, "What's Wrong with the Faith Movement?: E. W. Kenyon and the Twelve Apostles of Another Gospel." In the article, Hanegraaff spares no effort in portraying the Faith Teachers as greedy buffoons and making personal attacks not only on Copeland but others, including:

> John Avanzini. John Avanzini is billed by his Faith peers as a recognized authority on biblical economics. The truth, however, is that Avanzini is an authority on perverting Scripture as a means to picking the pockets of the poor. He has honed his craft into such an art form that when Faith teachers need money, they inevitably call on "Brother John." Armed with a bag full of Bible-twisting tricks, he tells the unsuspecting that "a greater than a lottery has come. His name is Jesus!. . ." When it comes to fleecing God's people, few can match the effectiveness of John Avanzini. There is an exception, however; his name is Robert Tilton.

> Robert Tilton. Robert Tilton hit the big time as a fisher of funds by developing a religious infommercial called "Success-N-Life. . ." It now appears that Tilton's ill-gotten gains may dwindle rapidly amid reports of scandal and a variety of lawsuits. [Here Hanegraaff repeats ABC's "Prime Time Live" charges that the prayer request letters Tilton promises to pray over end up in dumpsters instead.]

> Marilyn Hickey. Marilyn Hickey, much like Tilton, employs a broad range of tactics to manipulate followers into sending her money. . . for the most part, Hickey's tricks and teachings are recycled from other prosperity peddlers like Tilton, Hagin, and Copeland.[5]

Hanegraaff's attack on the Faith Teachers is not an isolated incident, it represents a broad and recurring assault. The attack on the Faith Teachers broadens the scope of the attack. Instead of marking an individual or a doctrine, this move is against a group of individuals who subscribe to a loosely defined body of thinking, the so-called Faith Teachings.

What Is a Faith Teacher?

The so-called Faith Teachers have been under attack for many years and from a broad spectrum of the Church. Sometimes their theology is referred to as "name it and claim it." The Faith Movement is sometimes called the "Word-Faith Movement." The fact is that there have been excesses among teachers in this area. Some individuals have gone too far and may, indeed, have made heretical statements.

But what really is the doctrine of the Faith Teachers? What marks a preacher as a Faith Teacher? When does one arrive at the point where he is a Faith Teacher? Is everyone who teaches on the biblical concept of faith to be considered a Faith Teacher?

Every evangelical preacher believes men and women must have faith. Faith is a necessary ingredient for salvation. Beyond that, evangelicals agree that people must "exercise" faith in God during their daily Christian walk. Pastors want their parishioners to exercise faith, to live lives of faith, to be faithful. What then, are Hanegraaff and others counseling us to avoid within "Faith" theology? We need to know precisely what the term "Faith Teacher" means.

Faith Teachers believe that Christians who know and understand the Bible can expect to experience real benefits from exercising faith. They can expect physical healing, emotional comfort, and increased prosperity in response to "walking in faith."

So the question is this: Is Hanegraaff wrong in calling Copeland the worst of all false teachers, is he wrong in calling all Faith Teachers cult leaders, and is he wrong in calling their "ardent followers" cultists? Is that an accurate assessment, or is it simply hyperbole that does not serve the cause of truth?

To answer those questions, we need to understand the nature of the specific charges against the Faith Teachers. Hanegraaff has identified what he calls "The Four Spiritual Flaws of the Word-Faith Movement."[6] Those flaws are: "Flaw #1: The 'Born-Again' Jesus Doctrine; Flaw #2: The 'Little Gods' Doctrine; Flaw #3: The Health and Healing Doctrine; [and] Flaw #4: The Wealth and Prosperity Doctrine." These four subject areas are probably better thought of as three by combining the last two on the list. This would give us three major teachings charged with being heretical: 1. Teachings on the Atonement of Christ, the "Born-Again Jesus"; 2. Teachings on the new nature of redeemed man, the "Little Gods" teaching; 3. Teachings about "health and wealth," the "Prosperity" teaching."

Before looking at each of those three areas, let me reemphasize the seriousness of the charges Hanegraaff and others have raised. He summarizes the failings of the Faith Teachers in general and Kenneth Copeland in particular this way:

> (In Word of Faith theology) God created the planet earth as a replica of the mother planet on which he lived, and he created Adam to be a god of this world in the same sense that God was a god of the planet on which he lived. . . Adam loses his godhood by committing cosmic treason. For the price of an apple he sells his godhood, God is kicked out of the universe and man takes on the nature of Satan.

> Now, that whole process is reversed when the Second Adam comes into being. There are various versions of how He comes into being. According to Kenneth Copeland he is visualized by God and then spoken into the womb of Mary, and arms, fingers, nails, and all of that come into existence, and finally, presto, there's Jesus Christ.

> Now, Jesus Christ lives the perfect life, and on the cross he becomes a Satanic being so that man can once again become a god. And as a god he can control his circumstances, including unlimited health and unlimited wealth.[7]

Do Hanegraaff and his colleagues, in this "synopsis"

of Copeland's doctrine, give us a fair picture of what all (or even any) of the Faith Teachers really believe? He certainly thinks he understands their doctrine, but I'm not sure he really does. And, if he does, I certainly don't think he represents it fairly and rationally.

I will now discuss the three major charges of heresy which have been leveled against the Faith Teachers.

Heresy Charge One: The "Born Again Jesus" Doctrine—What Really Happened in the Tomb?

One of the charges against the Faith Teachers is that they advocate a heretical position Hanegraaff has called "The Born-Again Jesus" doctrine:

> According to these false teachers, Jesus took on the very nature of Satan on the cross, died spiritually, and had to complete the plan of redemption in hell. . . they go on to say that after He defeated Satan and his minions in hell. Jesus emerged as a resurrected, born-again man.[8]

The subject here really is the nature, extent, method, and fruit of the Atonement of Christ. It addresses both the way the Atonement works as well as what it accomplished. Obviously this is a very complex theological subject. It is a subject that is as deep as the nature of God Himself and as broad as His intervention in the lives of men. If you were to ask the average pastor how Christ atoned for sin, he would say "by His death on the cross." That is the correct answer. However, if you were to ask a theologian for an explanation as to how the Atonement accomplished its work, you would get a much longer answer, for sure.

The Difficulty of Understanding the Atonement

One of the most scholarly attempts by CRI to prove that the Atonement theology of the Faith Teachers is heretical is a CRI article entitled, "The Atonement of Christ and the 'Faith' Message," by Brian Onken.

Onken admits that the subject is touchy. Of its complexity he says: "(God's) plans and counsels, infinite in majesty and wisdom, are not fully revealed to us—nor could they be."[9]

Onken quotes from theologian H. D. McDonald, who stresses the difficulty of fully understanding the atonement:

> Metaphor after metaphor is used to give some understanding of what Christ wrought in the cross. The feeling comes to us that there is more in the cross than can ever be put into words.[10]

Onken even warns us that we must be careful that we don't attempt to reduce all doctrine to a cast-iron system.

In an attempt to prove that Kenneth Copeland subscribes to a heretical Atonement theology, Onken quotes Copeland's talking about Jesus' decision to pay the price for sin:

> He (Jesus) made Himself obedient to death and put himself into the hands of God's enemy, Satan. Only He did it. He committed this act, not by treason, but by choice. He did it in order to pay the price for Adam's treason.[11]

Onken also has problems with Copeland's description of what happened to Jesus during the three days His body lay in the tomb:

> His (God's) purpose was to put Jesus through all the torments of hell. He bore our sins, our sickness, our disease, our griefs, our sorrow, and our pain. Then, at the command of God the Father, the Spirit of God came blasting down through the eons of time and injected the very "zoe" life, light, and glory of God into Jesus' spirit and He came out of that place victoriously![12]

Onken is adamant that the Faith Teachers are heretical. He says that it is "spiritually dangerous" to listen to them. Hanegraaff agrees with Onken wholeheartedly about the heretical nature of the Faith Teachers' Atonement theology. In a review of Benny Hinn's book, *The Anointing*, Hanegraaff writes:

> Hinn displays his ignorance of atonement theology

by confusing justification (Eph. 2:8-10) with sanctifica-
tion (Rom. 8:26-30) (14-15) and by repeating the heretical "ransom" theory of atonement—that Jesus had
to "buy back" an innocent humanity from the wicked
Satan (133) —refuted by Romans 5:9-21.[13]

But, have Hanegraaff and others demonstrated that
the Faith Teachers espouse heresy on the Atonement? I
don't think so. In fact, the heresy hunters may have merely
succeeded in making murky waters muddy.

What Happened in the Tomb?

What did happen during the Atonement? Is the "Ransom Theory" heresy? In attempting to understand the
Atonement, Christian thinkers have asked several questions: What degree of the separation within the Godhead
elicited Christ's dying cry, "My God, my God, why hast
Thou forsaken me" (Matt. 27:46 and Mark 15:34)? What
was the degree to which Christ was identified with our sin
on the cross ("For he hath made him [to be] sin for us,
who knew no sin; that we might be made the righteousness of God in him" 2 Cor. 5:21.)? What blessings accrue
to the redeemed as a result of the Atonement ("Christ
hath redeemed us from the curse of the law, being made
a curse for us: for it is written, Cursed [is] every one that
hangeth on a tree: That the blessing of Abraham might
come on the Gentiles through Jesus Christ; that we might
receive the promise of the Spirit through faith" Gal. 3:13-
14.)?

One of the graphic pictures the Faith Teachers continually return to is that of Jesus in hell, snatching the
keys of hell from Satan. This picture, the heresy hunters
maintain, is wrong. Jesus, they argue, certainly never went
to hell. Whether they are right or wrong about this may
be unprovable. However, for 2,000 years the Church has
formulated a confession that would lead one to believe
just that. The Apostle's Creed states that Jesus "Suffered
under Pontius Pilate, was crucified, dead and buried. He
descended into hell; the third day he rose again from the
dead."

Are the Faith Teachers heretical when they say that Jesus, during the time His body lay in the tomb, entered hell, and there defeated Satan? If they are heretics, then so are the Church Fathers who taught what we commonly refer to as the "classic" or "ransom" theory of the Atonement (which was held by the entire Church during its first thousand years.) *The Evangelical Dictionary of Theology* describes that theory in these words:

> In the early church there seems to have been little attention given to the way the atonement works, but when the question was faced, as often as not the answer came in terms of the (New Testament) references to redemption. Because of their sin, people rightly belong to Satan, the fathers reasoned. But God offered his son as a ransom, a bargain the evil one eagerly accepted. When, however, Satan got Christ down into hell, he found that he could not hold him. On the third day Christ rose triumphant and left Satan without either his original prisoners or the ransom he had accepted in their stead.[14]

So, is Hanegraaff justified in calling the ransom theory heresy? The broad base of the Church does not think so. No general support exists for such an exaggerated claim.

Historically, the Church has held to three theories of Atonement: the ransom theory; the satisfaction (or Anselmian) theory; and the moral influence (or Abelaradian) theory. *The New International Dictionary of the Christian Church* reiterates that all three of these theories (and others besides) have been believed by the orthodox Church:

The Christian Church has never accepted any one way of viewing the Atonement as the orthodox way. There is no doctrine of the Atonement equivalent to the two-natures doctrine in Christology, for example. The result is that there are many ways in which Christians have answered the question, "How does the death of Christ, long ago and so far away, save me here and now?"[15]

Many theologians regard Swedish theologian Gustaf Aulen as a consummate authority on Atonement thinking. In his book, *Christus Victor,* he makes the case that the ransom theory is the "typical view of the New Testament and the Fathers." He also says it is the theology revived by Luther during the Reformation. Describing this theory he says: "Its central theme is the idea of the Atonement as a Divine conflict and victory; Christ—Christus Victor—fights and triumphs over the evil powers of the world, the 'tyrants' under which mankind is in bondage and suffering, and in Him God reconciles the world to Himself."[16]

Unlike the heresy hunters, I am not sure which of the theories best explains the majesty and power of the Atonement, but I am reluctant to call any of them heretical. I do, however, agree with Aulen that there is something very magnificent about the ransom theory. It has, as he says, "drama." Christ victorious, saving men not only from the penalty of sin but from the foul grip of the oppressors of mankind. It is a theory a man can get his teeth into.

I think that is why the graphic picture of Christ's wresting the keys of hell from Satan's grimy grip appeals to the Faith Teachers. They are primarily men of action, not men of theories. They are men sweating over the bodies of infirm, weary, and ofttimes defeated Christians, calling them to healing, victory, and yes, even prosperity. The Faith Teachers, I believe, have connected intuitively—not by training—with a great biblical theme: "That God was in Christ, reconciling the world unto himself" (2 Cor. 5:19).

In speaking of man's need for a powerful God to ransom him from the chains of sin and fallen circumstance, the theologian William Horndern writes:

> Today we live again in a world where this ancient theme [the ransom theory of atonement] takes on new meaning. Modern man has a sense of being captured by fate, by powers beyond his control. He feels the tides of history bearing him, whether he will or no, to situations that he does not desire. . . in such a situation man needs, above all else, the good news that his enemies have been defeated. He needs to know that the forces of fate and the demonic intrud-

ers into life do not have the last word. This is still
God's world, and God has engaged the forces of evil
in mortal combat, and He has won. Christ is risen!
History is not a "tale told by an idiot" that signifies
nothing; it is the realm into which God has come and
demonstrated his sovereign power. Once more our
modern world can listen to Luther:

"And though this world, with devils filled,
Should threaten to undo us;
We will not fear, for God has willed
His truth to triumph through us"[17]

Heresy Charge Two: The "Little Gods" Doctrine

Anyone who listens to "The Bible Answer Man" regularly has heard Kenneth Copeland quoted on the subject
"little gods." Hanegraaff regularly ends the conversation
with a caller by cutting to a recording of Kenneth Copeland
or another Faith Teacher saying something apparently
foolish like: "Dogs beget dogs, cats beget cats, and gods
beget gods—You are all little gods!" It doesn't help when
these particular cuts display the speaker in his most irri-
tating voice.

At issue here is the discussion of what happens to us
when we are born again. The Faith Teachers do empha-
size that radical changes occur when the sinner becomes
a "saint." They believe that because the Bible declares, for
example, that we become a "new creature," we become a
new man, we no longer are slaves to sin.[18] The astounding
changes which take place are summarized by the Apostle
Peter in 2 Pet. 1:4: "Whereby are given unto us exceeding
great and precious promises: that by these ye might be
partakers of the divine nature, having escaped the corrup-
tion that is in the world through lust (2 Pet. 1:4)."

It is the frequent use of the concept of "divine nature"
that rightly worries the heresy hunters. If the Faith Teachers are suggesting that in partaking of the divine nature
we become God, then they have certainly violently dam-
aged the biblical teaching on the divinity of God. If the
Bible is clear on one thing, it is clear that in all the

universe there is but one God. All Judeo-Christian thinking hangs on this concept of monotheism.

Faith Teachers, the Eastern Orthodoxy, Mormons, and C.S. Lewis

Hanegraaff believes there is no difference between
what Copeland believes and what Mormons and New
Agers believe. He has stated that plainly:

> What I have just discussed with regard to "little gods"
> is only the tip of the insidious iceberg. . . but if you
> are going to welcome (the Faith Teachers) into the
> Church, please don't be two-faced. Welcome the Mor-
> mons, the Moonies, and the metaphysical practitio-
> ners.[19]

But not all CRI staff and contributors agree fully with
Hanegraaff on this point. One who has cautioned
Hanegraaff in this matter is Elliot Miller, Editor-in-Chief
of CRI's flagship publication, the *Christian Research Journal*. On "The Bible Answer Man," Hanegraaff and Miller
had the following exchange:

> (Hanegraaff): I remember when I first became presi-
> dent of the Christian Research Institute, you and I
> had quite a number of discussions about the Word/
> Faith theology. I, of course, at that point was very
> incensed about the fact that the Word/Faith Teach-
> ers, over and over again, say that redeemed man has
> the nature of God. They talk about us being little
> gods and I would say something like this to you,
> "Elliot, now this is really moving over into the king-
> dom of the cults and, you know, the Mormons tell us
> that we can become a god, but these people are tell-
> ing us that we are God" and yet, you cautioned me—
> and I think correctly so—not to just blanketly label
> these people as cultists—Why?

> (Miller): Because they have their own unique under-
> standing of what these terms mean. So there is a lot
> of orthodoxy within their teaching. In other words
> God is a personal God who did create the world, who
> is moral and holy, who gave us His law, who sent
> Jesus to die for our sins. In all of those respects they

are different from both the Mormons and the New Age Movement.[20]

Another scholar who does not think the Faith Teachers are in the same boat as the Mormons is Dr. Gordon R. Lewis, the highly respected Professor of Systematic Theology and Christian Philosophy at Denver Seminary. Lewis, who chairs the Philosophy of Religion department, writing in the *Christian Research Journal*, compared Mormon theology on the nature of God with Word-Faith theology:

> While it is true that these Word-Faith proponents speak of believers being "in the God class," they do not teach (as Mormons do) that "as man now is, God once was."[21]

While Lewis in no way endorses the overall theology of the Word-Faith Teachers in the article, he speaks in some detail to the "little gods" issue. He says that when Mormons quote Church Fathers to confuse Mormon theology with Christian theology, they do so incorrectly. For example, in the same article, Lewis quotes Ireneus: "If the Word became a man, it was so men may become gods."

But Lewis points out that Ireneus did not mean men may become God in an ultimate sense—in the way Mormonism teaches—but that we may become like God in some respects. Again, Lewis quotes Athanasius: "He indeed, assumed humanity that we might become God."

And again he states that they are wrong who would suggest that such out-of-context quotes indicate the Fathers were teaching "an eternal progression to a literal godhood."

Lewis cites the Eastern Orthodox doctrine of "deification," which is troublesome for many Western Christians. But Eastern Orthodox deification, Lewis notes, does not mean men become God in the way Mormons teach. He cites the Orthodox theologian Vigen Guroian:

> This does not mean that human beings are able to become God in his essence. But it does mean that they can become "gods" by grace even as they remain creatures of a human nature.[22]

Finally, Lewis responds to the Mormon claim that the late British Christian author C. S. Lewis taught Mormon theology:

> Did C. S. Lewis support an LDS (Latter-Day Saints) concept of deification? In *The Weight of Glory*, the imaginative writer uses figurative language to express the radical changes in believers from the dullest and most uninteresting persons in this life to "gods" and "goddesses" in glory. He must be understood metaphorically in view of his general defense of theism. Similarly, when in *Mere Christianity* he says we turn permanently into new little Christ's sharing God's power, joy, knowledge, and eternity, he is speaking in terms of our likeness to God being renewed. And in *The Screwtape Letters* his claim that God intends to fill heaven with "little replicas of himself" refers to replicas in certain qualities, not to becoming literal gods.[23]

The heresy hunters are wrong to try and make heretics out of people who speculate on what it eventually means for us to be partakers of God's divine nature by faith. The Faith Teachers are no more guilty of heresy than C. S. Lewis. Lewis, a man whom Evangelicals treat with the greatest respect, described his hope for the future this way:

> The command, "Be ye perfect," is not idealistic gas. Nor is it a command to do the impossible. He (God) is going to make us into creatures that can obey that command. He said (in the Bible) that we were "gods," and He is going to make good His words. If we let Him—for we can prevent Him, if we choose—He will make the feeblest and filthiest of us into a god or goddess, dazzling, radiant, immortal creature, pulsating all through with such energy and joy and wisdom and love as we cannot now imagine.[24]

What Do They Really Believe?

In spite of the fact that many Faith Teachers can be quoted out of context to prove they are polytheists, the fact is they are not. And I believe that anybody that listens to them in context will conclude they are not.

Do the snippets from Copeland's sermons prove he is a heretic? Do they prove that he believes—as Mormons do—that there is no essential difference between the nature of man and the nature of God? Finally, do they prove he believes—as New Agers do—that human beings actually are but an expression of the One Reality? I don't think so.

I believe he is trying to underscore what the Bible teaches: that when Jesus takes up residency within us, great spiritual changes take place and something happens to our humanity, namely that a new unsullied and godly nature is placed within us. I think he lays so much stress on the concept because he sincerely believes much of the Church has been cheated out of the benefits that derive from understanding our true identity in Christ.

Those who want to know what the Faith Teachers believe on this subject should ask them plainly. There is no need to sift through their old taped sermons and patch together a hypothetical theology. Benny Hinn, one of the Faith Teachers, spoke to his critics on this subject as early as 1990 on the Trinity Broadcasting Network. Before tens of thousands of people throughout the world via television he said:

> We're not God, we're the *children* of God. We're God-like in our spirit man. . . . They [those who accuse me of teaching that men are Gods] think we are saying we, in flesh, are God. We are not God in flesh. We are God-like in spirit. We are complete in Christ in spirit. Our spirit-man is God-like. It was birthed by God. It's a spirit being. That's what I'm talking about.

Heresy Charge Three: The "Health and Wealth" Doctrine

The hallmark of the Charismatic Renewal was the teaching that God desires to routinely invade the lives of His people in response to faith and prayer. The belief that God heals people today is not the issue. The issue is how and when he heals, and what role man's faith has in influencing or releasing that healing.

Now, at first glance, that does not seem to be such a

radical or divisive statement, but it is really at the heart of
the dialogue between the heresy hunters and the Faith
Teachers. I need to acknowledge that the issue certainly
is not black and white. Rather it is one of degree. For
example, Hank Hanegraaff has said on "The Bible Answer Man:"

> We cannot have unlimited health and unlimited wealth.
> While I believe in the perpetuity of spiritual gifts—I
> don't happen to embrace the theology that they ceased
> with the closing of the canon of scripture. . . [and] I
> must say that while I believe that God heals and that
> God heals today, while I believe that God is our pro-
> vision today, and while I think that God can prosper
> us today, I do not believe that God always heals.

Evangelicals admit that God does heal. They also
believe He providentially provides for the needs of His
people. But they disagree as to how, when, and under
what circumstances he does so.

When Does God Heal?

In some ways the issue smacks of the old Arminian/
Calvinist debate over the role of the sovereignty of God
and the will of man. Many Evangelicals fear that
Charismatics will misunderstand whether they are putting
their faith in a trustworthy God or in their own faith. In
1986, *Moody Monthly* magazine ran an article entitled,
"What's Behind the Prosperity Gospel," by Dr. James
Bjornstad, academic dean of Northeastern Bible College.
Bjornstad wrote: "When people are called on to place
their faith not in God himself but in laws that force God
to do their bidding, it strips God of his sovereignty and
his omnipotence (God cannot do what he wants)."[25]

But is that really what the leaders of the Faith Movement teach? The highly respected theologian and author,
Kenneth Kantzer, set forth the issues clearly in an editorial in *Christianity Today*. Kantzer thinks the Faith Teachers are well-meaning but wrong. He voices the concerns
of many when he suggests that the Faith Movement ". . .

makes false promises. These in turn lead to unscriptural desires for wealth and material prosperity, to false hopes for perfect physical health, and in the end to false guilt and despair."[26]

However, Kantzer is not willing to consign the entire Faith Movement to the ash heap of heresy. He suggests the Bible does teach that healing is part of God's provision in the work of Christ on behalf of the sinner. He writes:

> In a sense the Bible teaches healing in the Atonement. Scripture presents sickness as a part of the curse from which Christ redeemed us. Isaiah 53 affirms: "Surely he has borne our griefs and carried our sorrow" (v. 4). But the Hebrew can also be translated "surely he has borne our sicknesses and carried our pains." Verse 5 adds, "by his stripes we are healed." . . . as (theologian) Gordon Fee says, "Isaiah . . . refers first of all to the healings of the wounds of disease and sin. Yet, since physical disease was clearly recognized to be a consequence of the fall, such a metaphor could also carry with it the literal sense. . ."
>
> . . . God can miraculously break into our present sphere when he chooses, healing our bodies now in anticipation of the final healing.[27]

Kantzer goes on to say that Christians are divided as to when, and how, God decides to break into our present sphere. Some Christians, he says, believe that in the present age God only heals through secondary sources like doctors and drugs. But he admits that Scripture encourages us to pray for the sick. His compromise, he says, is that when his children became ill, he took them to the doctor, but he also prayed for them.

Does He or Doesn't He?

With all due respect, I believe Kantzer has hit the nail on the head. There are those who believe God virtually never heals (other than through secondary sources) and those who believe that physical healing is the normal expectation for faithful Christians. Their differences lie along a continuum. The problem is that if you are at one end of the continuum, it is very difficult to appreciate the position of the person on the opposite end. Word-Faith people may believe that Christians who are at the conservative end of the healing spectrum are totally faithless; Christians who have little expectation that God will "break into our present sphere" may look at the Word-Faith people as wackos.

It is true that intemperate statements have been made on both sides of the issue. Problems arise, however, when we become intolerant of those who do not see things the way we do. While I may honestly feel sorry for those Christians who believe God never heals, I cannot conclude that their brand of faith (or lack of faith) makes them heretics.

I am willing to agree that the Faith-Teachers have, on occasion, gone too far in their pronouncements, in their rhetoric, and in their sincere desire to raise the faith level of their congregations. Certainly, some Christian leaders go over the edge and preach things that are clearly extra-biblical and even dangerous. I think of the late Hobart Freeman, who became so hardened in his position on healing that he steadfastly advised his parishioners not to take any medication whatsoever. The result was that several women and children in his congregation died; he himself died before his time. Likewise, all of us have heard stories of Jehovah's Witnesses who die because they will not accept blood transfusions and Christian Scientists who die because they won't accept medical help. All of these extremes are to be avoided.

However, the heresy hunters have not demonstrated that men like Copeland, Hagin, Hinn, and the other Faith Teachers advocate such extreme measures. In fact, these men simply do not do so. The heresy hunters have yet to cite an instance where Copeland or the other prominent Faith Teachers have advocated that a sick person throw away his medicine. Yet I continually hear people say that that is what the Faith Teachers preach. Many Faith Teachers, on the contrary, will say something like this: "When God heals you, the doctors will know it!" Faith Teachers are also saddened when people pray in faith and nothing (apparently) happens. They often express great sympathy for those people who experience disappointment. They are unwilling, however, to stop praying for people because some are not healed.

Why Isn't Everybody Healed?

It is a fact that some people are not healed. Oral Roberts has said the first thing he wants to ask God when he gets to heaven is, "Why were they not all healed?" Kenneth Copeland resolves the problem this way:

> I am not the healer, God is the healer. I am the believer. It is my job to believe for healing. Don't ask me why people are not healed because I only do my job, not God's.

Faith Teachers believe God's provision applies to emotional and financial healing as well as physical healing. Again, it is certainly possible to point to excesses that have occurred in teachings about believing God for financial victory. It is also true that immature people attempt to put into practice principles they have heard taught but which they have not yet really understood. In those cases it is convenient to blame their immaturity on the teachers, but it is not always fair to do so.

The Faith Teachers think the Bible indicates that a faithful person should pray for God's direction and undertaking in every area of his life: He should pray over his fields and flocks if he is a farmer; he should pray over his inventory if he is a merchant; he should pray over his factory if he is a manufacturer. Faith Teachers believe God will routinely hear and answer these prayers.

In addition, Faith Teachers believe Christians should read what the Bible says about money and finances and practice the principles of generosity and giving. Faith Teachers believe people will be blessed for their obedience in this area as well as in others.

Excesses in the area of Faith Teaching should be condemned. Those who teach that all Christians should be rich or that God always heals are as aberrant in their thinking as those who teach that Christians should always be poor and that God never heals.

The Real "Prosperity" Doctrine of the Faith Teachers

The real message of the Faith Teachers is that men and women can expect God to respond to prayer. While God is sovereign and while He does know the end from the beginning, the Faith Teachers declare that God requires us to actively participate with Him in our faith-walk. They maintain that submission to the sovereignty of God does not mandate quietism. They teach that faith is an active relationship between man and God and must be exercised by an act of will.

Sometimes the Word-Faith Movement is called the "Positive Confession Movement." It is often likened to the New Age practice of positive confession. I will admit that some Christians have stepped over the line that divides legitimate Faith Teaching from perversions of it. But I do not believe the heresy hunters have proved that Copeland, for example, teaches what New Agers teach.

The difference is foundational. New Agers, who are Pantheists, see all reality as one. There is no difference between God and the "Universal Mind." They teach that we can tap into the Universal Mind and change external reality by what we believe. I do not think that the Faith Teachers believe that at all.

The Faith Teachers recognize that God stands outside time and space. They understand that we are His creatures. We have our existence in Him and are subject to Him. However, the Faith Teachers think God has made promises to us in His Word. They do not believe that faith is a matter of the mind but a matter of the spirit. And that is a distinction New Agers cannot make. The essence of faith theology is that the mind is carnal and unsubmitted to the things of God. They advocate that we must refuse to conduct our lives in accordance to the desires of our fleshly mind, we must read and believe the Word of God and submit ourselves to its thinking rather than our own thinking. That is a far cry from New Ageism.

One of the most Pentecostal Faith Healers, the late Charles S. Price, is well respected and often quoted by the modern Faith Teachers. Price contradicted the mistaken idea that faith is a matter of the mind and the metaphysical. In his book, *The Real Faith*, Price said:

> FAITH. . . I call it a grace because that is just what it is. In our blindness of heart and mind, we have taken faith out of the realm of the spiritual and, without realizing just what we were doing, have put it in the realm of the metaphysical. An army of emotions and desires has driven Faith from the chambers of the heart into the cold and unfruitful corridors of the mind.[28]

Kenneth Copeland apparently agrees with Price. During his 1993 "Believers Conference," he said, "Faith is not a mental force, it is a spiritual force!"[29] Copeland, in recounting a recent experience of his in believing for the physical healing of his wife, Gloria, said that he puts his faith not in his mental doubts and fears but in the Word of God: "God's Word, to me—the New Testament, to me—is His blood-sworn oath!"

Why Do People Listen to the Faith Teachers?

The Faith Teachers look around and see what they think is a Church filled with faithless people. In a sense, I believe they react the way Jesus did when the people brought the sick boy to Him. The boy's father said:

> Lord, have mercy on my son: for he is lunatic, and sore vexed: for ofttimes he falleth into the fire, and oft into the water.

> And I brought him to thy disciples, and they could not cure him.

> Then Jesus answered and said, O faithless and perverse generation, how long shall I be with you? how

long shall I suffer you? bring him hither to me. (Matt.
17:15-17; cf. Mark 9:17-27 and Luke 9:37-42)

The Faith Teachers remember Bible stories in which
trenches miraculously filled with water; they recall ax heads
that floated; they see God taking Elijah to heaven in a
chariot of fire. They remember the God of history who
says, "I am the God which healeth thee!" They see the
New Testament admonition to anoint the sick with oil,
pray for them, and believe they will be healed.

The heresy hunters, on the other hand, choose to
focus on the fact that some who hear the Faith Message
go too far with it. The heresy hunters relate stories about
people who believed in faith for a healing and, when it
never came, were devastated. The Faith Teachers respond
by pointing to the devastation that occurs when pastors
and Christians in general refuse to exert the simplest faith
for healing or to encourage their ailing congregations to
do so.

Many of the Faith Teachers marvel that the Church
often appears to be so lifeless. They can't comprehend
how the Church can meet broken people at the altar of
God and have so little to offer them. Believe me, I am not
suggesting that Christian counselors have no place in the
Church. But, just for a moment, I would ask the heresy
hunters to consider the fact that countless people in the
Faith Movement can bear testimonies of physical healings,
restored marriages, and financial miracles. They think
God healed them. They give Him the glory.

Of course, the heresy hunters can point to fraudulent
healers and real money-grubbing Elmer Gantrys and those
who traffic in the things of God. But they fail to balance
their remarks by pointing out that frauds are not found
exclusively in Pentecostal/Charismatic circles. There are
Fundamentalist fakes as was well as Pentecostal fakes;
there are mainline frauds as well as Charismatic frauds.
Obviously, one will not find fake faith healers ministering
in Fundamentalist churches which do not believe anyone
is ever healed!

   The end result of attempting to clean up the "messi-
ness" of pentecostal Christian experience is the same
today as it was in Jonathan Edwards' day: the revival
peters out. I think it is possible that history could mark
the decline and eventual end of the Charismatic movement with the end of the ministry of the Faith Teachers.
I pray that will not happen for the sake of the heresy
hunters, I hope they are not guilty of resisting something
God is promoting.

CHAPTER 8

Character Assassination

Some heresy hunters are willing to "kill the messenger" to prevent the spread of his message. A good example of this is the current effort by heresy hunters to discredit a few Christian ministers who believe Satanism is rampant in the United States. The heresy hunters are convinced that Satanism, while it may exist, is not a serious problem. The real problem with Satanism, they believe, is what they call "satanic panic"—exaggerated claims being made about Satanism by misguided Christian ministers such as Bob Larson, Johanna Michaelsen, and Mike Warnke.

Evangelical Christendom is divided on this issue. One viewpoint is that Satanism is reaching deadly proportions in the United States. Advocates of this position stress that Satanism frequently leads to ritual human sacrifice. Others, who disagree, maintain that reports of Satanism and satanic ritual abuse (SRA) are greatly exaggerated. They believe that satanic human sacrifice seldom, if ever, occurs.

Again, these two views represent the end points of a continuum. Thoughtful Christians need to approach the subject two ways: from the objective, rational examination of evidence, and from the exercise of scriptural discernment.

Both sides have made mistakes. Some Christians who sincerely believe the rise of Satanism is having disastrous effects on our nation, particularly among our youth, have sometimes written off all those who ask for evidence. These "true believers" sometimes think the skeptics are "unspiritual."

On the other hand, many Christians who debunk SRA see the people on the other side of the issue as "Satanic-fearing wackos." In their attempt to discredit what they believe is irrational thinking, the heresy hunters have been motivated to their most vicious attacks. These attacks represent the worst in Christian journalism.

While I don't intend to debate the SRA issue here, I do think I need to point out that United States' courts of law routinely convict people who say they killed in response to direction from the devil or demonic influence. One cannot deny that satanic murder occurs. People like Jeffery Dahmer and Richard Ramirez (the Night Stalker) do kill in the name of Satan. It is undeniable that the Matamoros, Mexico, drug ring certainly abducted and ritualistically murdered innocent victims to "raise the spiritual power." They believed these practices gave them power over the law enforcement agencies and prevented police from being able to stop the groups' criminal activities.[1] Human history, from ancient Babylon, to the Druids, to the Aztecs, tells us that human sacrifice always occurs in cultures that allow demons to be worshipped.

I believe the heresy hunters would at least agree that an occasional "satanic" murder occurs. They may even agree that it is at least theoretically possible that a person could be led into murderous Satanism from the larger world of the occult, or that one can graduate from lesser levels of witchcraft into Satanism. This, however, is something their secular colleagues refuse to admit. The non-Christian opponents to "satanic panic" think that Satanism is a rather harmless religious practice. They suggest that those who kill for Satan are simply crazy in the first place. They deny that satanists *become* murderers as a result of occult involvment.They point out that there are many "good" Satanists. As a matter of fact, Satanism is recognized today by the U.S. military as a "legitimate" religious practice. Many of the secular investigators of Satanism are themselves occult practitioners. They often deny that any connection exists between witchcraft and Satanism.

The entire dialogue about Satanism in America needs to continue. The truth about its nature and range needs to be documented. It is here that the heresy hunters do their worst damage: by vilifying the proponents of SRA, they reduce serious dialogue on the subject. Instead of debating the issue, they simply denigrate their opponents, but the very people they attack are the lone Christian voices in a secularized American wilderness. Heresy hunters, so intent in proving that reports of SRA are exaggerated, resort to completely discrediting those who disagree.

The problem, heresy hunters say, is not satanic crime. It's the "panic" caused by people who believe it is a national crisis. In their attempt to discredit the idea that Satanism is a genuine problem in America, the heresy hunters mount media campaigns designed to completely discredit the "SRA heretics."

Satanic Panic

Cornerstone, an avant-garde Christian magazine published in Chicago, is undeniably biased on the subject of Satanism in America. It takes the editorial position that satanic ritual abuse is primarily hysteria. In article after article, the editors make their position clear. The magazine not only publishes pieces that have a clear prejudice against the idea of widespread SRA, but it consistently attacks those who voice concern about it.

Perhaps the best example of *Cornerstone*'s bias was the article, "Satanic Panic," by Jon Trott. This exposé chronicled the criminal conviction of Paul Ingram, a Thurston County, Washington, sheriff. Ingram had been with the sheriff's department for sixteen years, had been the local Republican party chairman, and had run for the Washington state legislature. In 1988 two of his daughters accused him of sexually abusing them. Eventually two sons would also claim to have been ritualistically abused.

The girls also said they had undergone ritualistic abortions. Finally, Paul's wife, Sandra, also reported satanic rituals, including human sacrifices.

Ingram was arrested on 28 November 1988. Interestingly, he immediately called his pastor rather than an attorney. In May of 1989, Ingram pleaded guilty to six rape charges. A month later, however, he said his pastor had "led" him to imagine events that never occurred. Although he was allowed to change his plea, he was eventually sentenced to twenty years in prison.

Cornerstone editors see Ingram more as a victim than a criminal. They think that he was "counseled" into believing the charges made by four of his five children, as well as the corroborating testimony of his (now divorced) wife. They base that decision not on the opinion of the court but on the opinion of a specialist in cult mind control. In "Satanic Panic," *Cornerstone*'s Trott compares the Ingram prosecution to the witch-hunts of 1692 in Salem, Massachusetts. Trott is extremely skeptical of reports of widespread satanic ritual abuse. He also states that he believes reports of an underground Satanic network have no basis in fact: "The complete lack of evidence to support the existence of a satanic cult conspiracy leaves the honest Christian only one option: open-minded disbelief."[2]

Trott has also written that he does not believe children are being indoctrinated into Satanism by daycare workers or teachers.[3] He also stated his opinion that the stories of Satanic Ritual Abuse are mainly implanted in the minds of the alleged victims by prejudicial therapists:

> Satanic Ritual abuse is also rooted in, and validated by, therapists and mass media. There is absolutely no hard evidence to back the SRA stories of mass sacrifice, cannibalism, baby-breeding, and elaborate nationwide cult rituals.[4]

Cornerstone is passionately committed to its position that SRA is not occurring. It is fair to say that they are driven not only to disprove the existence of SRA but to also discredit those Christians who are sounding the SRA alarm. The magazine has devoted much of its energy to discrediting Christian books that report SRA, and the authors who write them.

Bob Larson

Cornerstone has also repeatedly attacked the well-known Christian radio personality, Bob Larson. Larson, host of the nationally syndicated talk show, "Talk Back with Bob Larson," is known for his vociferous stand against heavy metal rock music, Satanism, and SRA. After Larson recently published a novel that draws upon his conversations with alleged SRA victims, Jon Trott reviewed the book. His review attacks Larson's views on SRA and then turns the attack on Larson himself:

> If the reader wants a horrific roller coaster ride into hell—complete with vivid descriptions of human sacrifice and child sex—Bob Larson's newest contribution *Dead Air* (Thomas Nelson), is the ticket.
>
> The book's plot revolves around (surprise) a satanic cult that practices baby sacrifice, child rape and torture, and, of course, devil worship. . . . The book borrows freely from satanic ritual abuse victims' "testimonies" and reflects the worldview of the most wide-eyed believer in satanic cult conspiracies. . . .The writing quality is amateurish, the plot disgusting, and the reason for the book's existence baffling. . . . Larson clearly is inept in using fiction to tell the truth. I fear, however, that his inability to see the truth is the ultimate problem.
>
> Do yourself—and Christian publishing, a favor. Write a letter to Thomas Nelson (the publisher) expressing disgust with this new slasher/pornography genre in Christian books.[5]

Cornerstone published another unflattering article about Bob Larson that also displayed a decidedly anti-SRA bias. "Tickets to Nowhere: Another Counter-Cult Apologist Adventure, 'A Novelette Based on Fact'" was written by Gretchen Passantino. This article describes how Trott's review of *Dead Air* garnered him an invitation to confront

Bob Larson on CNN's "Larry King Live!" television show. Passantino's attitude in this article is one example of why I'm concerned about *Cornerstone*'s biased journalism. She recounts watching the program as it was broadcast live throughout the United States: "We, as Jon's fellow conspirators in the great SRB vs. SRS debate, [That's "satanic ritual believers" versus "satanic ritual skeptics"] viewed the program with delight."[6]

I wondered how she could view the spectacle of two evangelical Christians squaring off on national television as delightful.

In her description of the show and her account of what happened after it, Passantino demonstrated a flippant, sarcastic attitude. She says Trott called her from New York immediately after the Larry King show. Trott told her:

> As soon as Larry King was out of the room, Larson said, "Trott, you've got a really big SRCS (satanic ritual chip on your shoulder)!" . . . he says he's got evidence galore (in Denver) and I'm a chicken-liver if I don't go! I almost slipped out the door, but then he got me. . . the SRDDD—satanic ritual double dog dare![7]

Passantino uses the same tone throughout her piece. She describes her attempts to get Larson to open up his files on SRA to her. In what she apparently thinks was a humorous piece, she uses acronyms like these: ARASS (adult ritual abuse survivor syndrome specimen), the SRM (satanic ritual mess), the SRBH (satanic ritual bag holders), SRTS (satanic ritual "trash and slander"), SRTT (satanic ritual transcript tapes), SRPRG (satanic ritual prior restraint gambit), SNOT (satanic noise obscuring truth).[8]

Passantino ends "Tickets to Nowhere" by implying that those who believe satanic ritual abuse is occurring have resorted to vilifying people like herself, her husband, and Trott. Describing a television show she watched with her husband she says:

> It was Trinity Broadcasting. And—oh no!—there he

was, Mr. Larson himself. Next to him sat Hal and Kim Lindsay (sic) along with Johanna Michaelsen. They spent the next two hours vilifying "the critics,"—who us?—for being SISSY (stupid, ignorant, secret Satanist yahoos) because we kept on whining for evidence.[9]

From these quotes, you might get the impression that I think Passantino is a fool. Nothing could be further from the truth. I have had the pleasure of meeting her personally and ministering with her at a conference. I found her to be a very nice lady. However, I think something is wrong with her approach. I do not think such a sophomoric style, particularly the use of tasteless acronyms, is becoming to her. But most of all, I believe her approach typifies what I am trying to describe and combat in this book.

The heresy hunters need to stick to the issues. SRA is about whether people who get involved with the occult sometimes wind up committing satanic murder. To spend so much energy blackening the personal reputations of the people who believe in widespread Satanism is unworthy of *Cornerstone*. It diverges from the real point.

Passantino and her husband, Bob, should know better. They authored a book, *Witch Hunt*, that called for Christians to use tolerance and restraint when criticizing other Christians. The jacket cover of the book (which, ironically, also is published by Thomas Nelson, publisher of *Dead Air*) says:

> Many Christians today, in their concern for preserving orthodox Christianity, are actively attacking heresy—or what they perceive to be heresy—within the church. Although the threat of heresy is real, many genuine Christians are being falsely accused. Because of faulty reasoning and a lack of biblical discernment, Christians are striking out against Christians.

However, it seems when the subject is satanic ritual abuse, witch-hunting is allowed. For example, the Passantinos allege that their opponents want to "change the justice system so recovered 'memories' alone can bring convictions in criminal court."[10] I am unaware that such an agenda is widespread among those who are warning us about Satanism. What I hear people saying is that satanic ritual abuse is occurring and that it needs to be taken seriously. I do not believe any serious opponent of SRA wants anyone convicted on testimony brought by a lone accuser.

The Anti-Satanic Inbreeding

Those who downplay SRA's existence find themselves, perhaps unwittingly, teamed up with secular forces who not only hate the Christian message on Satanism but who are also unfriendly to Evangelical Christianity itself. Bob Larson, at the 1993 conference of the National Religious Broadcasters, made charges that some Christian journalists were trading stolen documents with secularists. He said Jay Grelen, who co-authored a story on Larson for *World* magazine, not only "received stolen documents," but had harassed Larson's staff members. In a press conference Larson stated that he was told Grelen was out to get him. Larson said he was told that Grelen boasted, "having brought Mike Warnke down," he was going to "get" Larson as well.[11]

Larson suggests that there is "a free flow of information exchange" between Christian reporters and secular reporters. Christian reporters, he says, even trade information with enemies of the Church, including Satanists. He cited, as an example, one religious broadcaster who trafficked in potentially damaging private papers that had been surreptitiously obtained from the Larson ministry: "Instead of sending those transcripts to me as a brother in Christ and asking me about them, he saw fit to photocopy them and send them—at least in one case—to an unbeliever who was a noted harasser of Christian ministries, who then sought to bring further harm to our ministry."[12]

One Christian researcher, Richard Phelps, is concerned about this propensity for Christian journalists (especially in the area of SRA investigation) to traffic with the secular world:

It becomes very obvious in the Passantinos' articles on Satanic Ritual Abuse (SRA) in both the *CRI Journal* and *Cornerstone*, along with those authored by Jon Trott in *Cornerstone*, that a strong presuppositional bias [exists] which filters out any otherwise credible evidence for SRA. . . psychology journals critical of therapist evidence for SRA are cited [in their writings], along with the scientific materialist publication *The Skeptical Inquirer*, and the ultra-liberal *The Village Voice*. In Jon Trott's article, "About the Devil's Business," in issue 93 of *Cornerstone*, he cites *Satanism in America* as credible evidence for the non-prevalence of SRA, even though the authors of that book are a collection of secular humanists, neo-pagans, and a Wiccan! . . .completely absent are any positive references to long-standing Christian individuals and ministries that have worked with SRA victims, such as Dr. Carl Raschke, National Information Network; Exodus San Antonio, Jacob Aranza; and many others too numerous to mention. The Passantinos are Associate Editors for *Cornerstone* and contributing editors for the *CRI Journal*.[13]

If that sounds a little harsh, it isn't. The Passantinos routinely represent the secular world's position on this issue. In fact, Gretchen Passantino allowed herself to be introduced on the Fox Television Network as the head of an organization whose purpose is to debunk the notion that Satanism is an organized force. Those who report being ritually abused, Passantino said, were simply giving psychologists what they wanted to hear—what she called "unsubstantiated, directive, contaminated, therapeutic testimony."[14] In other words, when people come forward and say they were ritually abused in satanic ceremonies, Passantino thinks they are doing so simply because counselors and psychologists are leading them to believe those things happened to them when, in reality, they did not.

Cornerstone attacked Larson's character in a particularly destructive way. In one article, it suggested his approach to ministry is more led by business interests than spiritual ones and intimates that he is really into the SRA discussion for its dramatic appeal:

> An anti-rock crusader in the sixties and seventies, Bob [Larson] switched in the early eighties to fighting cults. Next came talk-show radio. . . in 1985, Larson expanded his ministry offices from five thousand to fifteen thousand feet. 1989 was a banner year for Larson. He published five books that year, among them *Straight Answers About the New Age* and, more significantly, *Satanism: The Seduction of America's Youth*. Larson increasingly focused on Satanism and, as Geraldo and others discovered, Satanism and "satanic ritual abuse" made for great media drama.[15]

Bob Larson reaches thousands of teen-agers for Christ each year. I wonder if his detractors ever simply listen to his show and try to put themselves in the place of a kid who is beset by a culture that is nearly insane with drugs, perverse sex, crime and, yes, Satanism.These hardened kids tune in to a tough guy who will tell them straight-out that their choice is heaven or hell. It's the "turn or burn" message. Maybe it doesn't play well among the sophisticated, but it may be just what it takes to affect the audience Larson is attempting to reach.

It's hard for me to believe that Larson's critics are not touched when one of these hopeless, helpless kids gives his life to Jesus on the air. It makes you wonder if the heresy hunters aren't the ones who need a reality check.

Mike Warnke

Cornerstone's determination to oppose everyone who rings the SRA alarm has escalated during the past few years. Perhaps the best (or worst) example of that was their article: "Selling Satan: The Tragic History of Mike Warnke." The *Cornerstone* article on Warnke is gigantic—nearly 30,000 words (almost two thirds the size of this book) with more than 150 footnotes. It is an impressive piece of work, authored by Jon Trott and Mark Hertenstein. The secular press was certainly impressed with the article. The *Chicago Tribune* ran an article by a freelance writer who compared Trott and Hertenstein to Bob Woodward and Carl Bernstein, the *Washington Post* duo who toppled President Nixon during the Watergate years. Ironically, the *Chicago Tribune* article also compared them to another secular journalist: "Trott and Hertenstein have assumed a watchdog role that has often been left for those in the mainstream press, such as Diane Sawyer of ABC's 'Prime Time Live.'"[16]

Regardless of *Cornerstone*'s underlying motives for their strongly skeptical position on SRA, the magazine was very honest about its reason for running the Warnke story. It targeted Warnke precisely because he spread the SRA rumors. In the third paragraph of the Warnke story we read:

> A generation of Christians learned its basic concepts of Satanism and the occult from Mike Warnke's testimony in *The Satan Seller*. Based on his alleged Satanic experiences, Warnke came to be recognized as a prominent authority on the occult, even advising law enforcement officers investigating occult crime. We believe *The Satan Seller* has been responsible, more than any other single volume in the Christian market, for promoting the current nationwide "Satanic scare."[17]

Cornerstone launched an all out search into Warnke's background, his life-style, and his finances in an effort to discredit him. They found what they were looking for. There were some real reasons for concern about the Warnke ministry. Perhaps the most damning information was that, during twenty years of ministry, he had been divorced three times. This, of course, calls into question the wisdom of his continuing in Christian ministry. Most Christians would agree that such marital instability probably disqualifies him or at least demands strict attention and correction. Certainly such information signals a call for ministry to Warnke in hope of bringing healing to him.

But *Cornerstone* was uninterested in seeing Warnke healed. They wanted him out of ministry. Why? One can only wonder if the magazine would have gone to the same expense and trouble to track down the entire past history of a Christian rock star who had failed in his personal life. Nevertheless, *Cornerstone* spared no energy in the search to prove that Warnke was a fraud from start to finish. They found high school and college acquaintances who called upon their thirty-year-old memories to describe what he was like as an unsaved youth. *Cornerstone*'s conclusion: Warnke was a habitual liar who was never a Satanist. He made up his story, including his account in *The Satan Seller*, to get position, standing, and ministry. The magazine characterized his entire ministry as one lie after another, picturing him as a man totally lacking in virtue. *Cornerstone* concluded their massive diatribe by saying: "Mike (Warnke) has sinned against the public for years. . . there is no way for him to have done the things he claimed in *The Satan Seller*."

Trott and Hertenstein also said they did not feel that they needed to talk to Warnke before they published the article:

> Some of our readers will expect us to have followed the steps Matthew 18:15-17, starting with a private confrontation. This passage gives Christ's instructions on what to do "if your brother sins against you," and the process stops if the brother repents privately.[18]

Although they did call him and summon him to an airport meeting on the eve of publication, they contend that they did not need to meet with him privately. They also said that since others had confronted Warnke in the past, they were relieved of the responsibility of doing so. They said they did not have to pursue the biblical admonition of Matthew 18 because:

> This is not a private dispute between Mike Warnke and a magazine. A public figure is susceptible to public scrutiny and criticism. Matthew 18 is not violated when public figures are publicly rebuked. (However, other scriptures are violated if the rebukes being made are not fair, true, or applicable to the person.)[19]

It may be technically correct that Matthew 18 was not violated. I have wrestled with that question and am not sure just how that passage is best interpreted in the television age. I do understand Trott's and Hertenstein's point. It might well be that it is not necessary to meet with Christians and pursue Matthew 18 guidelines every time you write an article or a book that disagrees with a brother or shows him in a bad light. However, I believe when you write 30,000 words that are designed to remove a man from ministry forever, some one-on-one is warranted.

The heresy hunters, by and large, are in complete agreement that private confrontation does not have to occur when one criticizes public ministries or Christian books. However, I believe Trott and Hertenstein violated their own test of "fairness." I am concerned about the sheer volume of the charges brought against Warnke, the personal nature of the charges, and the mixing of his personal and doctrinal problems. The debate about satanic ritual abuse is a separate issue from questions about Warnke's personal life. The validity of claims about SRA do not rest on whether or not Warnke made up his story of his involvement with the occult.

The Satan Seller, in spite of what *Cornerstone* says, is hardly a source book for those who say SRA is occurring. In the first place, it describes events that occurred nearly thirty years ago. It describes Warnke's description of his six-month involvement in Satanism. But the personal lives of Warnke and Larson are not the issue. Whether or not they are adulterers or rip off artists does not prove or disprove that SRA is occurring.

On the other hand, few would dispute that Warnke was a powerful minister. Few would dispute that he effectively preached an orthodox gospel to tens of thousands of people. What we do know is that Warnke's approach to ministry was unusual. He was billed as a "Christian comic." The primary tool of a comedian is exaggeration. Warnke has admitted that he has exaggerated his story, especially in his comedy acts. However, he steadfastly maintains that the basic elements are true. Warnke has submitted his entire ministry to an outside board of respected ministers. This independent advisory council issued a five-page report of their findings after investigating Warnke's conduct. They concluded that while Warnke has made mistakes, *Cornerstone* treated him very unfairly and harmed him. They said:

> A careful review. . . has proven that the original article by *Cornerstone* was less than fair in representing the truth and some editorial bias slanted the reporting of the facts "behind the story." However, regardless of the fact that extensive damage has been inflicted by the *Cornerstone* article, the Council has determined to take a positive approach in an attempt to salvage whatever possible future there may be for Warnke Ministries.[20]

But the truth is that there is no future for Warnke Ministries. This unique ministry, which needed help and correction, has instead been destroyed. It is too late to fully restore Warnke's ministry; the damage is too deep, the accusations too widespread.

Cornerstone, in proving that Warnke exaggerated his story and had moral lapses, can take satisfaction in knowing that they have brought the guilty to justice. And maybe justice was served; we cannot be pleased when a minister of the gospel lives a ragged-edged life.

But then why do I feel so bad about it? Perhaps one reason is that I remember the one time I saw Warnke perform. It was in Idaho Falls, Idaho, during the time I pastored there. When he came to Idaho Falls, a young member of my church came to me and asked me if I would interview Warnke for a local newsletter. I went to the meeting with preconceptions and some misgivings. Frankly, from what I knew, Warnke was "not my cup of tea." I was not into "Christian comedy."

However, I saw a "real" man who told of his struggles in a way with which I could identify. In addition, his preaching gave me genuine spiritual insight. In fact, he touched me deeply. After the show I went backstage to interview him. He was not feeling well, so we cancelled the interview, and I really never got to talk with him.

But I can't help remembering the kids who gave their hearts to Christ that night. I can't help thinking of the tens of thousands of kids who made commitments to Christ under Warnke's solid teaching.

When I read the *Cornerstone* article, I did what few people will do—I checked it out in detail. I reread *The Satan Seller*. I compared the details in the book with the details in the *Cornerstone* article. My own independent research confirmed what the independent board of ministers said: *Cornerstone* was less than fair, was biased, and did irreparable harm to Warnke. It was not an article designed to rescue an erring brother. It was an article designed to destroy him. And it did just that.

Trott and Hertenstein went to the Christian Booksellers' Association convention in Dallas shortly after their article was published. Copies of *Cornerstone* were inserted into exhibitors packets. The article was widely distributed. Press coverage focused on Warnke.

Soon people began coming to Warnke concerts armed with the *Cornerstone* article, waving it in the faces of people who had come to hear him. Before long his crowds of thousands had dwindled to a handful.

Maybe Trott and Hertenstein were right to do what they did. God will judge. Maybe the Kingdom has been served. Maybe the Christian in-depth journalist is the minister of the future. I just don't think so.

Maybe the discrediting of men like Larson and Warnke somehow proves that Satanists do not put people to death in black rituals. I just don't think so.

I seriously wonder what the heresy hunters believe they have accomplished.

CHAPTER 9

Sins against the Body

In A.D. 325, three hundred bishops of the Church from throughout the Roman Empire assembled in Nicaea at the request of Emperor Constantine. Together, they hammered out the Nicene Creed, which still stands as a bulwark against doctrinal error. They also condemned the theology of Arius, who espoused a Christology very similar to that of modern Mormons and Jehovah's Witnesses.

According to Eastern Orthodox tradition, during the council St. Nicholas of Myra was so incensed by the unorthodox claims of Arius that he actually struck him in the face. The rest of the bishops, who were astonished at this action, had Nicholas put in jail and sought to deprive him of his office.

I'm impressed that the bishops, although they voted unanimously to excommunicate Arius, understood that they must treat him with respect. Nicholas' action—the smiting of Arius—was as important to the bishops as Arius' heresy.

Ministry Should Be Reasonable and Charitable

Modern heresy hunters should learn from the Council of Nicaea. When they determine a man is a heretic, they seem to think it is all right to slap him repeatedly and publicly. What they miss is that all legitimate ministry is aimed at restoring people. When the attack turns from what a man does or says to who he is, we have moved from ministry to inquisition.

For example, Hinn (along with his Holy Spirit) is called a buffoon; Copeland is told he does not belong in the Body of Christ; Schnoebelen is called a liar; Tilton is revealed as a money-grubber; Charismatics appeal only to their experience and not to scripture; Larson is charged with only being interested in building a financial empire; Warnke is accused of fabricating his entire life. All of these men were "struck in the face."

This is not simply a question of procedures. The problem is deeper than that. Somehow the heresy hunters must come to the realization that ministries should be treated with a minimum standard of respect.

Heresy hunters should address the real issues; they should not have a hidden agenda. If, for example, the heresy hunters have a problem with the fact that Benny Hinn blows on people and they fall over, they must address that. If the real problem is that Hinn claims people are healed when they are not, then address that issue. Similarly, if Bob Larson's and Mike Warnke's statistics on SRA are wrong, the heresy hunters should challenge them about that. If the real problem with Bob Larson is his fund-raising tactics, then be honest and confront him on that issue.

What Is the Reason for the Attack?

Sometimes heresy hunters forget that ministry is about people. We preachers are in the business of restoration. *Cornerstone* magazine, if it were really interested in Mike Warnke's personal life, could have corrected him without ruining his life. The editors could have shown him the article they eventually published and said, "We are going to publish this if you don't make some meaningful changes in your life-style." Or, they could have told him they were going to publish unless he agreed to meet with a board of respected Christian ministers. Or, third, they could have sent their research to a respected group and asked them to address Warnke.

The argument they mounted to explain why they did not do that is weak. They simply said "others have talked to him in the past and he didn't respond." That may be true, but others did not publish a 30,000 word diatribe about him. If the information revealed in the article was powerful enough to force Warnke to make changes, then it could have done so without holding him up to public ridicule.

Again, it isn't so much that the heresy hunters have failed to follow some legalistic requirement (such as meeting personally with him in advance of publishing their story). The issue is that their real motivation is to end the ministries of certain individuals. The Tanners want Schnoebelen out of ministry; *World* magazine wants Larson off the radio; and Hanegraaff wants Copeland and Hinn removed from television.

Attack the Doctrine, Not the Man

It is possible to talk about people without being vindictive. A number of years ago, Dave Hunt and T. A. McMahon wrote *The Seduction of Christianity*—a Christian best-seller. They were able to write a book that was controversial and confrontive, but, in my opinion, free from the rancor I see in the heresy hunters. The book created a furor and led to a spate of other books, responses like *The Reduction of Christianity* and follow-ups like *Beyond Seduction*. When *The Seduction of Christianity* was published in 1985, Dave Hunt was on everybody's list; people thought he was either the greatest or the worst critic of the Church in twenty years. One of the reasons for the excitement was that he dared to "name names."

Faith Teachers like Kenneth Hagin, Kenneth Copeland, Robert Tilton, and Charles Capps were named. So were people like Norman Vincent Peale and Robert Schuller. In addition, Hunt quoted from the books and tapes of those with whom he disagreed. However, in retrospect, it is clear that Dave Hunt conducted himself with a measure of restraint that is a world apart from the vindictiveness of the heresy hunters of the 1990s. Consider these words of conciliation in his introduction:

> In the following pages we quote from the books and sermons, as well as the radio, television, and seminar talks, of a number of influential Christian leaders, both men and women, past and present. Many are sincere and dedicated servants of the Lord whose lives and ministries influence millions. . . it should also be understood that those whom we name. . . are mentioned only to provide documentation and to show the extensiveness of the seduction. We would caution readers not to judge specific individuals but rather the teachings and practices that are being pointed out. This is not a hairsplitting theological treatise.[1]

Throughout his book, Hunt repeatedly states that he is interested in what the men and women are teaching, not in who they are. He does not judge them. He leaves that to God. There are no searching probes into the ministers' personal lives or into the financial arrangements of their ministries; he leaves that to their denominations, governing boards, and law enforcement agencies. Rather, he disagrees with their doctrines. He simply cites what they have said and describes why he disagrees with them. They are not charlatans to him, they are simply wrong. In fact, he empathizes to such an extent that he says those who teach wrong doctrines are, themselves, victims.

In many ways, the heresy hunters of today really believe they are following in the footsteps of men like Hunt and the late Walter Martin. However, I believe the heresy hunters have missed the real heart of the genuine apologists. They have attempted to copy the process, but some of the data didn't get transferred. They go through the same motions, but the message is garbled.

Today's heresy hunters, though they think of themselves as scholars, are really more like vigilantes. They search out those who look guilty and carry out "justice," not at the end of a rope but at the tip of a pen. They are

not simply investigators, nor do they stop at being pros-
ecutors; they see themselves also as judges and execution-
ers.

Who Are the Heresy Hunters, Anyway?

There is one important question that I believe the
Church of the 1990s must answer. Since we live in the age
of the thirty-second sound bite, we may need to ask ourselves, "Are the heresy hunters themselves accountable to
anyone?" Who decides when and where they will strike?
They are very quick to point pious fingers at men and
women who are healing the sick and driving out demons,
but who authorized them to accuse the brethren?

It is essential for ministries that are not under attack
to answer this question because they may be next on the
heresy hunters' lists. Heresy hunters represent a danger
to the Church. I hope that influential ministers will be
stirred to challenge unwarranted attacks and come to the
defense of besieged brethren. I can understand why a
minister would be reluctant to do this. For one thing, one
exposes oneself to attack.

But we must understand that the feeding frenzy un-
leashes a wild excitement in the heresy hunters. No one
is safe. No minister is so careful in his every word that he
cannot be accused of heresy if he gets on the wrong side
of these people. The Spanish Inquisition stands as a his-
torical warning for those complacent enough to think "It
can't happen to me." It can.

I wrote this book not only to describe heresy hunting
but also as a brotherly rebuke to those who engage in it.
I call them to repentance with these words from Isaiah:

> Woe unto them that call evil good, and good evil; that
> put darkness for light, and light for darkness; that put
> bitter for sweet, and sweet for bitter!

> Woe unto [them that are] wise in their own eyes, and
> prudent in their own sight! (Isa. 5:20-21)

One Thing Is Lacking

The heresy hunters seem to lack an important quality—the fear of God. They take the mantle of ministry too lightly. The Bible teaches us that:

> Promotion [cometh] neither from the east, nor from the west, nor from the south. But God [is] the judge: he putteth down one, and setteth up another. (Psm. 75:6-7)

The heresy hunters do not walk with fear when it comes to laying hands on men and women of God. That is a source of wonder to me. Do they totally disdain the anointing of God?

I realize that abuse of power exists in the Church. And it is true that cult-leaders sometimes take refuge in what they call "The Anointing." However, that does not mean we should not respect the call of God upon the life of a minister. David was reluctant to lay hands on Saul. He, indeed, refused to touch the Lord's anointed. It is that missing reluctance, that lack of mercy, that most troubles me about the heresy hunters.

William Shakespeare spoke of mercy this way:

> "The quality of mercy is not strain'd;
> It droppeth as the gentle rain from heaven
> Upon the place beneath. It is twice blest:
> It blesseth him that gives and him that takes." *The Merchant of Venice*

My Response to the Heresy Hunters

Responding to the heresy hunters has been difficult for me. I have written about this subject without relish because I am too aware that I, like them, at times fall far short of the highest level of Christian conduct. Our common condition is "miserable, and poor, and blind, and naked" (Rev. 3:17).

I have not entered the fray with eagerness. I believe I have been drawn into it by the sight of wounded colleagues who have fallen under "friendly fire." I could no longer call myself a Christian soldier if I avoided the battle. Sadly, however, I realize with David, that these actions make me a man of war and one who has shed blood (1 Chron. 28:3).

I take consolation in this: I know that both I and the heresy hunters will one day sheathe our swords for good. The time is coming when we will make war no more. Until that day, I pray they will gain the wisdom to turn from attacking the Body and join the real battle we must all wage together against the forces of darkness.

Chapter Two

1. ABC News, "Prime Time Live," (21 November 1991) Transcript #220.

2. Word of Faith World Outreach Center, et al., v. State of Texas (Austin, TX: 18 March 1992), Civil No. A-92-CA-089, 6.

3. Word of Faith World Outreach Center, et al., v. State of Texas (Austin, TX: 25 June 1992), Civil No. A-92-CA-89, 23.

4. An audio tape of this program is available by writing to Word of Faith, P. O. Box 81900, Dallas, TX 75381. Ask for "Response to 'Prime Time'" tape #1218C.

5. Eric Slick, "From the Publisher," *Tulsa Christian Times* (October 1992): 2.

6. Larry J. Sabato, *Feeding Frenzy: How Attack Journalism Has Transformed American Politics* (New York: MacMillan, Inc., 1991), 1.

7. Ibid., 6.

8. Alan Bloom, *The Closing of the American Mind* (New York: Simon and Schuster, Inc., 1987), 25-26.

9. "Death of Fetus Results in Murder Conviction," *Boise Statesman* (12 December 1991).

10. Richard N. Ostling, "What Does God Really Think About Sex?" *Time* (24 June 1991): 49.

11. Ibid.

12. Ibid., 50.

13. Neil Postman, *Amusing Ourselves to Death* (New York: Penguin Books, 1985), 8.

14. "Trinity Prof Attacked for Resurrection Teaching" *Christianty Today* (11 November 1992): 62.

15. Millard Erickson, et al., "Report of the Ad Hoc Committee to Examine the Views of Dr. Murray J. Harris" (9 February 1993)

Report on file in the office of the president of Trinity Evangelical Divinity School.

16. "Special Update on the Controversy with the Evangelical Free Church," Witness Inc. News (March, 1993), 1.

Chapter Three

1. "Preliminary Statement on Benny Hinn," #DP-073 (San Juan Capistrano, CA: Christian Research Institute, 23 July 1992).

2. "The Bible Answer Man," tape on file with author.

3. Randy Frame, "Same Old Benny Hinn, Critics Say," *Christianity Today* (5 October 1992): 53.

4. Randy Frame, "Best-Selling Author Admits Mistakes, Vows Changes," *Christianity Today* (28 October 1991): 44.

5. Harold O. J. Brown, *Heresies* (New York: Doubleday & Company, 1984), 1.

6. Ibid., 196.

Chapter Four

1. "The Bible Answer Man" radio show (6 October 1992), tape on file.

2. Stephen F. Cannon, M. Kurt Goedelman, and G. Richard Fisher, "Benny Hinn's Anointing: Heaven Sent or Borrowed," *Personal Freedom Outreach Journal* (July-September 1992): 14.

3. Robert Bowman, "A Summary Critique: Good Morning, Holy Spirit," *Christian Research Journal* (Spring 1991): 36-37.

4. Randy Frame, "Best-Selling Author Admits Mistakes, Vows Changes, "*Christianity Today* (28 October 1991): 44, 46.

5. Randy Frame, "Same Old Benny Hinn, Critics Say," *Christianity Today* (5 October 1992): 54.

6. Cannon, et al., "Benny Hinn's Anointing," 2.

7. Benny Hinn, *The Anointing* (Nashville: Thomas Nelson Publishers, 1992), 27-28.

8. Frame, "Best-Selling Author," 44.

9. "Benny Hinn," *Publishers Weekly* (10 February 1992): 44.

10. Frame, "Best-Selling Author," 44.

11. Ibid.

12. William Alnor, "Leading Charismatic Denies the Historic Doctrine of the Trinity on National Television," photocopied news release dated 12 October 1990 in possession of author, 1.

13. William Alnor, 2.

14. Frame, "Same Old Benny Hinn," 54.

Chapter Five

1. Stanley M. Burgess and Gary B. McGee, *Dictionary of Pentecostal and Charismatic Movements* (Grand Rapids: Zondervan Publishing House, 1988), 326, s.v. "fundamentalism."

2. Richard Pierard, "Lausanne II: Reshaping World Evangelism," *Christian Century* (16-23 August 1989): 740-742.

3. John F. MacArthur, Jr., *Charismatic Chaos* (Grand Rapids: Publishing House, 1991), 26.

4. Ibid., 27.

5. Ibid., 37.

6. Ibid.

7. Ibid., 57.

8. Ibid., 31.

9. Ibid., 43.

10. Ibid., 21.

11. Ibid., 244.

12. Ibid., 239-242.

13. Ibid., 77.

Chapter Six

1. James Spencer, *"The Attack on Mormonism's Temple of Doom,"* (Boise, ID: Through the Maze).

2. Jerald and Sandra Tanner, *The Lucifer-God Doctrine* (Salt Lake City: Ut.), 16.

3. Ibid., 4.

4. Ibid., 5.

5. Dawn House, "LDS Reviewing Abuse Claims: Satanic Rituals Copy Sacred Ceremonies," *Salt Lake Tribune*: (25 October 1991): A1.

Chapter Seven

1. "The Bible Answer Man" (6 October 1992) radio show, tape on file.

2. "Bibliography on the Faith Movement," No. DP-075 (San Juan Capistrano, CA: Christian Research Institute, July 1992).

3. "The Bible Answer Man" (6 October 1992) radio show, tape on file.

4. "Bibliography on the Faith Movement."

5. Hank Hanegraaff, "What's Wrong with the Faith Movement?" *Christian Research Journal* (Winter 1993): 20.

6. Hank Hanegraaff, "Documentation for 'Christianity in Crisis,'" No. DP-159 (San Juan Capistrano, CA: Christian Research Institute, May 1991): 1-5.

7. "The Bible Answer Man" (6 October 1992).

8. Hanegraaff, "Documentation for 'Christianity in Crisis,'" 1-2.

9. Brian Onken, "The Atonement of Christ and the 'Faith' Message," *Forward,* 7,1 (n.d.):9.

10. Ibid.

11. Ibid., 10.

12. Ibid., 11.

13. Hank Hanegraaff, "A Summary Critique: The Anointing," *Christian Research Journal* (Fall 1992): 38.

14. Walter A. Elwell, ed., "Theories of the Atonement," *Evangelical Dictionary of Theology* (Grand Rapids: Baker Book House, 1984): 101.

15. J. D. Douglas, ed., *The New International Dictionary of the Christian Church* (Grand Rapids: Zondervan Publishing House, 1978): 83, s.v. "atonement."

16. Gustaf Aulen, *Christus Victor* (New York: The MacMillan Company, 1961), 4.

17. William Hordern, *The Case for a New Reformation Theology* (Philadelphia: Westminster Press, 1959), 144-145.

18. See: 2 Cor. 5:17, Gal. 6:15, Eph. 4:24, Col. 3:10, and Rom. 6:16-22, King James Version.

19. "The Bible Answer Man" (6 October 1992).

20. Ibid.

21. Gordon Lewis, "A Summary Critique: Are Mormons Christians?" *Christian Research Journal* (Fall 1992): 36.

22. Vegen Guroian, "The Shape of Orthodox Ethics," *Epiphany Journal* (Fall 1991): 9.

23. Lewis, "A Summary Critique, What's Behind the Prosperity Gospel?" 36.

24. C. S. Lewis, *Mere Christianity* (New York: MacMillan, 1974), 174-175.

25. James Bjornstad, *Moody Monthly* (November 1986): 19-20.

26. Kenneth S. Kantzer, "The Cut-rate Grace of a Health and Wealth Gospel," *Christianity Today* (14 June 1985): 14.

27. Ibid., 14-15.

28. Charles S. Price, *The Real Faith* (Plainfield, N.J.: Logos Books, 1972), 5.

29. Kenneth Copeland, TV broadcast of "The Believer's Voice of Victory" on 4 April 1993.

Chapter Eight

1. James R. Spencer, "Satanic Ritual Abuse: Is It Occurring?" *Update*, 92-1, (1992). Publication of Through the Maze Ministries, Jim Spencer, president/founder.

2. Jon Trott, "Satanic Panic," *Cornerstone* (Issue 95): 12.

3. Jon Trott, "There Is a Devil," *Cornerstone* (Issue 95): 3.

4. Jon Trott, "The Grade Five Syndrome," *Cornerstone* (Issue 96): 18.

5. Jon Trott, "A New Genre: Christian Porn," *Cornerstone* (Issue 95): 18.

6. Gretchen Passantino, "Tickets to Nowhere," *Cornerstone* (Issue 96): 10.

7. Ibid., 14.

8. Ibid.

9. Ibid.

10. Bob and Gretchen Passantino, "Hard Facts About Satanic Ritual Abuse," *Christian Research Journal* (Winter 1992): 21.

11. Bob Larson, press conference at the conference of National Religious Broadcasters, held in Los Angeles, Calif., in February 1993, video on file.

12. Ibid.

13. Richard Phelps, letter on file.

14. Gretchen Passantino, "Sightings" (6 November 1992), video tape on file.

15. "Bob Larson's Ministry Under Scrutiny," *Cornerstone* (Issue 100): 37.

16. Joe Maxwell, "Religious Write," *Chicago Tribune* (28 December 1992), Section 5, 1.

17. Jon Trott and Mike Hertenstein, "The Satan Seller," *Cornerstone* (Issue 98): 7-8.

18. Ibid., 30.

19. Ibid.

20. Rev. Richard Morgan, et al., "Advisory Council Report" delivered to Warnke Ministries, Burgin, Ky. (11-12 January 1993): 1.

Chapter Nine

1. Dave Hunt and T. A. McMahon, *The Seduction of Christianity* (Eugene, Oreg.: Harvest House, 1985), 9.

TRINITY BROADCASTING NETWORK DIRECTORY OF TBN-OWNED AND AFFILIATE STATIONS

(• indicates affiliate station)

ALABAMA

- • Birmingham Ch. 51
- • Decatur Ch. 22
- Dothan Ch. 41
- • Florence Ch. 57
- • GADSDEN Ch. 60
- • Huntsville Ch. 67
- • MOBILE Ch. 21
- • MONTGOMERY Ch. 45
- • Opelika Ch. 35
- Scottsboro/
- Huntsville Ch. 64
- Selma Ch. 52
- Tuscaloosa Ch.46

ALASKA

- • Anchorage Ch. 22
- • NORTH POLE Ch. 4

ARIZONA

- Bullhead City Ch. 20
- Cottonwood Ch. 58
- Flagstaff Ch. 62
- Globe Ch. 63
- • Lake Havasu Ch. 25
- PHOENIX Ch. 21
- Quartzsite Ch. 43
- • Safford Ch. 17
- Shonto/Tonalea Ch. 38
- • Sierra Vista Ch. 33
- Tuscon Ch. 57
- Tuscon Ch. 56

ARKANSAS

- • DeQueen Ch. 8
- Fayetteville Ch. 42
- Ft. Smith Ch. 27
- • Harrison Ch. 66
- • Little Rock Ch. 33
- Mountain Home Ch. 43

CALIFORNIA

- Alturas Ch. 30
- Atwater/Merced Ch. 57
- Bakersfield Ch. 55
- Buellton/
- Solvang Ch. 53
- Coalinga Ch. 42
- Desert Hot Sprgs. Ch. 40
- Eureka Ch. 47
- • Fresno Ch. 56
- • FRESNO Ch. 53
- Lancaster/
- Palmdale Ch. 54
- • Lompoc Ch. 23
- Mariposa Ch. 28
- Monterey Ch. 53
- Palm Springs Ch. 66
- Porterville/
- Visalia Ch. 15
- Redding Ch. 65
- Ridgecrest Ch. 27
- Sacramento Ch. 69
- • Sacramento Ch. 21
- • SAN JOSE Ch. 65
- • San Luis Obispo Ch. 36
- SANTA ANA Ch. 40
- Santa Barbara Ch. 15
- • Santa Maria Ch. 65

Thousand Oaks Ch. 55
Twnty-Nine Palms Ch.38
Ventura Ch. 45
Victorville Ch. 33
• Vista Ch. 49

COLORADO
• Boulder Ch. 17
• Colorado Sprgs. Ch. 43
Denver Ch. 57
Denver Ch. 47
Denver Ch. 33
Loveland Ch. 48
• Pueblo Ch. 48

DELAWARE
Dover Ch. 67
• Wilmington Ch. 26

FLORIDA
Dunedin/
Clearwater Ch. 60
Ft. Meyers Ch. 67
• FT. PIERCE Ch. 21
• Gainsville Ch. 69
• JACKSNVILLE Ch. 59
Lake City Ch. 23
• LEESBURG/
ORLANDO Ch. 55
• Marietta Ch. 55
• Melbourne Ch. 62
MIAMI Ch. 45
Naples Ch. 58
Okeechobee Ch. 19
• Panama City Ch. 38
Pensacola Ch. 63
Port Charlotte Ch. 56
• Sarasota Ch. 24
Sebring/
Vero Beach Ch. 17

St. Petersburg/
Tampa Ch. 18
• Tallahassee Ch. 17
• W. Palm Beach Ch. 47

GEORGIA
Albany Ch. 23
ATLANTA Ch. 63
Augusta Ch. 65
Brunswick Ch. 33
• DALTON Ch. 23
• Hazelhurst Ch. 63
Luella Ch. 19
Savannah Ch. 67
• Thomasville Ch. 22
Tifton Ch. 17
Valdosta Ch. 54
Waycross Ch. 46
Waycross Ch. 39

HAWAII
• HONOLULU Ch. 26
• KONA Ch. 6

IDAHO
Boise Ch. 47
Coeur d' Alene Ch. 57
Pocatello 15
Twin Falls Ch. 16

ILLINOIS
• Bloomington Ch. 64
Champaign/
Urbana Ch. 34
Decatur Ch. 29
Elgin Ch. 30
• LaSALLE Ch. 35
• Marian Ch. 27
Palatine Ch. 36
• QUINCY Ch. 16

MISSISSIPPI

Biloxi Ch. 29
• *Bruce* Ch. 7
Clarksdale Ch. 31
Columbus Ch. 25
Greenville Ch. 33
Grenada Ch. 25
Jackson Ch. 56
• *Jackson* Ch. 64
McComb Ch. 36
Natchez Ch. 58
Pascagoula Ch. 46

MISSOURI

• *Branson* Ch. 25
Columbia Ch. 56
• *Joplin* Ch. 9
• *Monett* Ch. 38
• *Neosho* Ch. 32
Poplar Bluff Ch. 39
Springfield Ch. 52
St. Charles Ch. 34
• *ST. JOSEPH* Ch. 16
St. Louis Ch. 18

MONTANA

• *Billings* Ch. 14
Great Falls Ch. 53
Helena Ch. 41
Kalispell Ch. 26

NEBRASKA

• *Council Bluffs/*
Omaha Ch. 45
Lincoln Ch. 39
Norfolk Ch. 52
Ogallala Ch. 26

NEVADA

Carson City Ch. 19
Las Vegas Ch. 57
Reno Ch. 45

NEW JERSEY

Atlantic City Ch. 36

NEW MEXICO

• *Alamogordo* Ch. 29
• *ALBQUERQUE* Ch. 23
• *Carlsbad* Ch. 63
• *Clovis/Hobbs* Ch. 65
• *Farmington* Ch. 47
• *Maljamar* Ch. 46
• *Portales* Ch. 66
Raton Ch. 18
• *Roswell* Ch. 27

NEW YORK

Albany Ch. 64
Binghampton Ch. 14
• *BUFFALO* Ch. 45
• *Geneva* Ch. 38
Glens Falls Ch. 14
Jamestown Ch. 10
• *Massena* Ch. 20
Olean Ch. 22
POUGHKEEPSIE Ch. 54
• *Rochester* Ch. 59
• *Syracuse* Ch. 59
Utica Ch. 41

NORTH CAROLINA

• *Asheville* Ch. 41
Charlotte Ch. 68
• *Charlotte/*
Gastonia Ch. 62
Durham Ch. 56
Fayetteville Ch. 53
Goldsboro Ch. 59
• *GREENSBORO* Ch. 61
Greenville Ch. 54
Jacksonville Ch. 21
Lumberton Ch. 52
Raleigh Ch. 38

Statesville Ch. 66
Wilmington Ch. 20

NORTH DAKOTA
- Bismarck Ch. 29
Fargo Ch. 56
Grand Forks Ch. 22
- Rugby Ch. 20
Williston Ch. 40

OHIO
CANTON Ch. 17
Chillicothe Ch. 40
- Columbus Ch. 24
Dayton Ch. 68
Kirtland Ch. 51
Lexington Ch. 32
- Marietta Ch. 26
- Marion Ch. 39
Portsmouth Ch. 21
- SANDUSKY Ch. 52
- Seaman Ch. 17
Springfield Ch. 47
- Toledo (North) Ch. 68
- Toledo (South) Ch. 46
Youngstown Ch. 39
Zanesville Ch. 36

OKLAHOMA
Ardmore Ch. 44
- BARTLESVILE Ch. 17
- Guymon Ch. 53
Lawton Ch. 27
OKLAHOMA CTY Ch. 14

OREGON
Bend Ch. 33
Coos Bay Ch. 33
- Eugene Ch. 59
Grants Pass Ch. 59
Klamath Falls Ch. 58
Lakeview Ch. 21

Medford Ch. 57
- PORTLAND Ch. 24
Roseburg Ch. 14

PENNSYLVANIA
Erie Ch. 44
- Kingston Ch. 54
Meadville Ch. 52
Pittsburgh Ch. 65
- Scranton Ch. 26
State College Ch. 42
Williamsport Ch. 11

SOUTH CAROLINA
Anderson Ch. 18
Beaufort Ch. 40
Charleston Ch. 44
- Columbia Ch. 51
Georgetown Ch. 54
- GREENSVILLE Ch. 16
- Greenville Ch. 58
Myrtle Beach Ch. 66
Orangeburg Ch. 52
- Spartenburg/
Greenville Ch. 66

SOUTH DAKOTA
Aberdeen Ch. 20
Arlington/
Huron Ch. 38
Brookings Ch. 15
Huron Ch. 38
Madison Ch. 27
Montrose/
Mitchell Ch. 63
Rapid City Ch. 33
Sioux Falls Ch. 52
Sioux Falls/
Rowena Ch. 51
Yankton Ch. 31

TENNESSEE

Cookeville Ch. 46
Farragut Ch. 66
• Greenfield Ch. 2
• HOLLY SPRGS Ch. 40
Jackson Ch. 35
• Knoxville Ch. 60
Knoxville Ch. 32
• Memphis Ch. 65
Morristown Ch. 31
• Nashville Ch. 36
• NASHVILLE Ch. 50

TEXAS

Abilene Ch. 51
Abilene Ch. 57
• Amarillo Ch. 20
Austin Ch. 63
• BEAUMONT Ch. 34
• Big Springs Ch. 30
Brownwood Ch. 26
College Station Ch. 57
Corpus Christi Ch. 57
DALLAS Ch. 58
• HARLINGEN Ch. 44
• HOUSTON Ch. 14
• Huntsville Ch. 31
• Kerrville Ch. 2
• Killeen Ch. 31
Kingsville Ch. 47
• Livingston Ch. 66
Lubbock Ch. 53
• Lufkin Ch. 5
• ODESSA Ch. 42
Palestine Ch. 17
Paris Ch. 42
Port Lavaca/
Victoria Ch. 62
San Angelo Ch. 19

• Temple Ch. 53
Uvalde Ch. 15
Victoria Ch. 43
• Wichita Falls Ch. 26

UTAH

Ogden Ch. 64
• Salt Lake City Ch. 36
Vernal Ch. 39

VERMONT

Burlington Ch. 16

VIRGINIA

• Charlottesville Ch. 58
• Danville Ch. 18
• Harrisonburg Ch. 24
Lynchburg Ch. 32
Norfolk Ch. 24
• Richmond Ch. 67
Roanoke Ch. 49
Virginia Bch. Ch. 24
• Woodstock Ch. 10

WASHINGTON

Aberdeen Ch. 23
• Ellensburg Ch. 39
Longview Ch. 36
• Richland Ch. 49
SEATTLE/
TACOMA Ch. 20
Spokane Ch. 55
Spokane Ch. 57
WENATCHEE Ch. 27
Yakima Ch. 64

WEST VIRGINIA

• Charleston Ch. 45
• Huntington Ch. 19
Parkersburg Ch. 39

WISCONSIN

Green Bay Ch. 68
Janesville Ch. 19

TBN RADIO STATIONS :

KTBN SUPERPOWER SHORTWAVE RADIO
   8 A.M. - 6 P.M.
(P.D.T.)
   15.590 MHz.
   6 P.M. - 8 A.M.
(P.D.T.)
   7.510 MHz.
(Reaching Around the World)
RADIO PARADISE ST. KITTS, WEST INDIES
   830 KHz. A.M.
HOQUIAM, WASHINGTON
   KGHO AM 1490
   KGHO FM 95.3

INTERNATIONAL STATIONS:

NEVIS, W.I.
   Charlestown Ch. 13
• GRAND CAYMAN IS.
   Georgetown Ch. 21
• HAITI
   Port-au-Prince Ch. 16
ST. LUCIA
   Castries Ch. 13
• BELIZE
   Belize City Ch. 13
• COSTA RICA
   • San José Ch. 23

   • Santa Elena Ch. 53
   • Limon Ch. 23
   • Cerro de la Muerte Ch. 53
• EL SALVADOR
   • San Salvador Ch. 25
• HONDURAS
   • Tegulcigalpa Ch. 57
NICARAGUA
   • Managua Ch. 21
   • Quiabu Ch. 15
   • La Gateda Ch. 27
• ARGENTINA
   • Buenos Aires Ch. 66
• BOLIVIA
   • La Paz Ch. 27
CHILE
   Valpariso Ch. 32
ITALY
   Milano Ch. 11
   Porto Ceresio Ch. 46
   Como Ch. 39
   Varese Ch. 33
   Ponte Tresa Ch. 39
   Luino Ch. 44
   Nosate Ch. 41
   Novara Ch. 59
   Ivrea Ch. 36
   Biella Ch. 59
   Borgo Franco Ch. 28
   Castletto Crvo. Ch. 28 & 68
   Pavia Certosa Ch. 41
SWITZERLAND
   Locarno Ch. 37

Lugano/
Campione Ch. 44
GREECE
Athens Ch. 62
Corinth Ch. 54
Macedonia Ch. 62
• ALBANIA (gov't. owned)
• ICELAND
• Reykjavik Ch. 45 & 53
RUSSIA
St. Petersburg Ch. 40
CISKEI, S. AFRICA
Bisho Ch. 24
TRANSKEI, S. AFRICA
Umtata Ch. 67
Butterworth Ch. 25
Ngangelizwe Ch. 67
Mt. Ayliff Ch. 27
Queenstown (under const.)
Port St. Johns (under const.)
Engcobo (under const.)
Mt. Fletcher (under const.)
• ZAMBIA
• Lusaka
• SWAZILAND
• Mbabane
• NAMIBIA
• Windhoek
• LESOTHO
• Maseru
• BOPHUTHATSWANA
• ZAIRE
• Kinshasa

• REPUBLIC OF SOUTH AFRICA
(SABC)
• TV 1 - Ch. 13
• TV 2 - Ch. 9

For more information, please write:

TBN
P. O. Box A
Santa Ana, CA 92711
24-hour Prayer Line: (714) 731-1000

James R. Spencer
Biographical Information

Rev. Jim Spencer is a Christian author and lecturer. He formerly pastored an Evangelical church in Idaho Falls, Idaho, for nine years.

He is the author of three previous books:
- *Beyond Mormonism: An Elder's Story* (Chosen Books)
- *Have You Witnessed to a Mormon Lately?* (Chosen Books)

> This book was a finalist for the Evangelical Press Association's Gold Medallion Award for Evangelism.

- *Hard Case Witnessing: Winning "Impossibles" for Christ* (Chosen Books)

Rev. Jim Spencer has published articles in many leading Christian magazines, and he co-authored the movie *The Mormon Dilemma* with Ed Decker. Prior to entering the ministry, he enjoyed a broad business background, including working on several newspapers and as a news writer for Associated Press.

A recognized expert on religious cults, Jim Spencer has appeared on radio and television, including the Trinity Broadcasting Network, Bob Larson's "Talk Back," and the late Dr. Walter Martin's "The Bible Answer Man." He lectures throughout the country on cults and the occult, and secularism.

Jim Spencer lives in Boise, Idaho, with his wife of 27 years, Margaretta. He has three daughters.

What Others Have Said About Jim Spencer's Work:

• *I know Jim Spencer and his heart . . . His is a dynamic ministry*
> —Dr. Walter Martin, Author, *Kingdom of the Cults*

• *James Spencer challenges Christians to volunteer for service in the war against atheism and pantheism*
> —Dr. Gorden R. Lewis,
> Denver Conservative Baptist Seminary

• *Jim's spirit is not argumentative, yet he is authoritative*
> —Jack W. Hayford, Senior Pastor,
> The Church on the Way, Van Nuys, Calif.

• *Jim Spencer has the ability to see through the smokescreen of deception and strike a blow for freedom*
> —Ed Decker, Author, *The God Makers*